How Many Needless Deaths in the Middle East Before Trump Is Allowed to Meet with Putin Again?

EIR Contents

www.larouchepub.com   Volume 45, Number 20, May 18, 2018

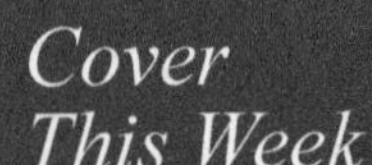

Cover This Week

kremlin.ru

Presidents Putin and Trump meet on the sidelines of the G-20 Summit, July 7, 2017.

HOW MANY NEEDLESS DEATHS IN THE MIDDLE EAST BEFORE TRUMP IS ALLOWED TO MEET WITH PUTIN AGAIN?

If Roosevelt Had Lived

May 10—Coming amidst the completely unprecedented developments of the recent weeks, yesterday's celebration of V-E Day in Moscow, and particularly President Putin's deeply moving tribute to those who unstintingly gave all to defeat the Nazis, call to mind our American President, Franklin Roosevelt, who had succumbed, worn out, just weeks before the final defeat of Nazism. Roosevelt's death at that moment cheated that generation out of the promise of the postwar world, and the postwar America, for which he had so long planned and fought.

Lyndon LaRouche's New Delhi address of Dec. 3, 2008, "The Time Has Come for a New System," in which he again proposed the "Four-Power Agreement," reproduces Franklin Roosevelt's thinking of back then, through the prism of LaRouche's more advanced concepts up through the present.

Lyndon LaRouche said, "We have to have a coalition of forces on the planet, which is strong enough, and understands its mutual self-interest sufficiently, to restore the kind of control which the United States attempted to promote under Franklin Roosevelt. Roosevelt, in dealing with China, and dealing with the Soviet Union, and other countries, toward the end of the war, said, you don't have to *like* the other country; you don't have to *like* its government; you don't have to *like* its policy. What you have to do, is establish an international system of control, under which you don't have things running loose, which are menaces. Simply having treaty organizations or similar things tantamount to treaty organizations, where people have such an interest in maintaining the treaty organization that they will regulate themselves and their own country. And you can get cooperation on this."

This was the way in which Roosevelt intended to compose a postwar world with Stalin's Russia, China, and India. But his successor, Harry Truman, offered to meet Stalin just as soon as he could come to the United States—which he well knew Stalin would never do. The model for postwar Germany was to be what we have seen in Austria—neutrality freed from foreign military occupation. A united Germany would have flourished—but that was not to be. The Korean War, which has loomed over us from its beginning in 1950 until the present moment, offered Stalin a way to punch back against Anglo-American military pressure in Europe, through an unguarded back-door in Asia. In retrospect, another sort of nightmare followed after World War II, because Roosevelt died and his plans and ideals were buried with him by British imperialism.

Within his proposed four-power agreement, LaRouche proposed using the uniqueness of the U.S. Constitution to anchor the issuance of massive amounts of credit-generation for productive investment, emphasizing infrastructure. There is no way to set about transforming the millions of unskilled labor in India, for example, into skilled labor, without massive infrastructure creation.

Back then, in 1945, we had failed to create the postwar world which our heroes expected and deserved. Instead of that bright promise, we spent an entire lifetime under the threat of nuclear war—a threat which persists today. But today, a new alternative is opened thanks to Lyndon LaRouche's creative vision, centered in the Belt and Road Initiative launched by China's President Xi Jinping, which over one hundred countries have joined in with.

Today, Mahathir Mohamad, at age 92, was re-inaugurated as Prime Minister of Malaysia 15 years after he last left that position, becoming the world's oldest elected leader. Mahathir Mohamad is very well-known internationally for his open agreement with Lyndon LaRouche, for instance, concerning George Soros. He assumes office as a world leader who is a Muslim, who is also a foremost partisan of the Belt and Road initiative, which he said today he had suggested in detail in a personal letter to President Xi Jinping. Today, our phones are ringing off the hook with people calling to tell us how important Mahathir Mohamad's fight for the Belt and Road is for the Middle East, which is being threatened by dangerous proxy warfare. It's true. The Belt and Road is the answer for Southwest Asia—as Lyndon LaRouche has proposed for over 40 years, and as Franklin Roosevelt would agree.

ZEPP-LAROUCHE WEBCAST

As Tensions Mount, Keep an Eye on the Big Picture

This is the edited transcript of the May 9, 2018 Schiller Institute New Paradigm webcast, an interview with the founder of the Schiller Institutes, Helga Zepp-LaRouche. She was interviewed by Harley Schlanger. A video of the webcast is available.

Harley Schlanger: Hello. I'm Harley Schlanger of the Schiller Institute. Welcome to our weekly international webcast, featuring our founder and President, Helga Zepp-LaRouche. Today is May 9, celebrated in many countries, including Russia and Israel, as Victory Day, to commemorate the end of the fighting of World War II in Europe. We hope that as you join us in commemorating this day, you reflect on the horrors of war, but also redouble your commitment to work with the Schiller Institute, to find peaceful solutions to the crises in the world today.

We have some new, unfolding crises, starting with President Trump's speech last night in which he announced that he's taking the United States out of the Joint Comprehensive Plan of Action, the nuclear weapons agreement with Iran. Helga, this is quite a significant event, but we don't know the full implications. What does it mean and what are the reactions to it so far?

Helga Zepp-LaRouche: There is general concern voiced by many countries and forces, for example, China and Russia, but also Merkel, Macron, and May. They have all expressed concern that this is potentially a very dangerous development, because it could easily spin out of control. It's a quite complicated situation. Iran's President, Hassan Rouhani, said that if the other participants in the agreement—China, Russia, France, Germany, and Great Britain stick with it, then Iran will comply and continue with the agreement. That may turn out to be difficult, first of all because the internal situation in Iran is not so easy. Some hardliners have said that they will abandon the treaty. The Speaker of

Xinhua

Iranian President Hassan Rouhani, seen here with Foreign Minister Javad Zarif, said if the remaining participants in the 2015 nuclear deal continue with it, then Iran will.

Xinhua/Ahmad Halabisaz

Iranian Parliament Speaker Ali Larijani

official photo

U.S. Ambassador to Germany, Richard Grenell

Prime Minister of Israel Benjamin Netanyahu at the UN, 2016.

the Parliament, Ali Larijani, said that other hardliners were already shouting "Death to America." That looks complicated and dangerous.

Then there is the threat by the new American Ambassador in Berlin, Richard Grenell, who on his first day at his post, immediately issued a threatening tweet: "German companies doing business in Iran should wind down operations immediately." That was not met with enthusiasm. Wolfgang Ischinger, former German ambassador to United States, tweeted back a very diplomatic response: "My advice, after a long ambassadorial career: Explain your own country's policies and lobby the host country—but never tell the host country what to do, if you want to stay out of trouble." There were commentaries in such publications as *Spiegel Online*, saying that Trump's unilateral cancelling of the treaty is shaking the very foundations of the Western Alliance.

It remains to be seen what will ensue. Trump has said that he wants to get rid of this deal because it's a very bad deal, and that he has another one. Unfortunately, he has not yet given any indication what that plan would be.

The Chinese daily newspaper *Global Times* and also the VIPS, the Veteran Intelligence Professionals for Sanity, a group of retired intelligence people from the United States, have warned that if Iran were to now go back to its nuclear program in response, then this could immediately trigger a spiral of competition in an arms race, in which Saudi Arabia, Egypt, and Turkey all might want to start, or actually would start their own nuclear weapons programs. There is great concern about how Trump's announcement will affect ongoing

preparations for the summit between President Trump and Kim Jong-un of North Korea. President Trump's Iran announcement ties in to all of these matters.

The reactions from the military are quite different. The majority of the military in both the United States and Israel do not share the views expressed by Israeli President Benjamin Netanyahu. Unfortunately, Trump seems to have adopted Netanyahu's views. In the United States, the Secretary of Defense, General James Mattis, and the Chairman of the Joint Chiefs of Staff, General Joseph Dunford, have said that Iran was complying with the Agreement. Some people in the Israeli defense establishment have said the same thing.

On the other hand, Netanyahu has some cabinet ministers who are quite wild. Upon the election victory of Hezbollah in Lebanon, these cabinet members commented that if Syria's President Assad doesn't kick Iran out of Syria altogether, they would "liquidate" Assad! This is bellicose language. As Trump was speaking, cancelling U.S. participation in the Iranian deal, a new air strike hit near Damascus. No one has yet claimed responsibility, but the likelihood that the perpetrator was Israel is very high, since that nation had previously launched a similar missile attack.

That means we face a very dangerous and very messy situation. President Trump says he has an alternative plan. That plan needs to have certain key elements to be viable. Any peace plan, or any security architecture, has to take into account the security interests of all participating countries. Iran was adamant about

U.S. Defense Secretary James N. Mattis giving Congressional testimony in Washington, D.C., May 9, 2018.

developing its own nuclear weapons not only to defend against what happened to Saddam Hussein in Iraq and Muammar Qaddafi in Libya, but also because Israel has nuclear weapons—which nobody speaks about but which is a known, public secret. So any agreement, for it to work, must also include a security guarantee for Iran.

Given the condition of the entire Middle East and Southwest Asia, after the destructive wars in Iraq, Libya, Syria, Yemen, and Afghanistan, it is very clear that the only way that this region's problems can be solved, is what I have said many times: You need the extension of the New Silk Road into the entire region, from Afghanistan to the Mediterranean, from the Caucasus to the Gulf, and you need an integrated development plan for all of these countries as a whole. This will only work if Russia, China, India, Iran, Egypt, the United States, and hopefully European countries, all agree that this region must be economically built up. The only way peace will come to this region, the only way that to rid the region of terrorism, is to move forward with a perspective of hope for the future.

So, I really hope that President Trump does indeed have an alternative, more comprehensive plan, and that it includes joint ventures of the United States, Russia, China, and India in the development of this region. A beginning was made between China's President Xi Jinping and India's Prime Minister Narendra Modi when they met in Wuhan, China a week ago, where they agreed to start joint development projects in Afghanistan, building a railroad that will travel through Iran, Afghanistan, Tajikistan, Kyrgyzstan, and China. That would be the beginning of many other projects to follow. You need a comprehensive development plan for it to work. I really hope that President Trump is thinking in that direction, because that's the only way that part of our world can be stabilized.

Schlanger: Let me just probe a couple of areas you brought up, because some things are really quite significant. You talked about the effect of sanctions. The effort to use sanctions as, in a sense, almost an act of war, doesn't only affect the country that's being sanctioned. Congressional sanctions against Russia, the so-called CAATSA—Countering America's Adversaries Through Sanctions Act—has profound implications for Germany, especially with regard to gas and pipelines. The latest sanctions, as you mentioned, was the U.S. Ambassador to Germany threatening German firms. Is

there a reaction coming from Europe, and especially from Germany on this?

Zepp-LaRouche: I know that German industry is demanding that the German government and the EU protect it. If sanctions against Iran are declared, such action would also hit German and European firms currently doing business in Iran. On top of the sanctions against Russia—this is getting to be too much! This is why some of these commentaries are saying that this is shaking the very foundations of the Western Alliance. Just a couple of a days ago, the eastern division of German industry issued an appeal to the German government and the EU, saying that the recent round of sanctions against Russian oligarchs and firms is already costing German industry several hundred million euro in direct losses, and much more in indirect losses. This goes to the very existence of many firms, whose entire production lines are threatened.

Look at the danger of German firms or European firms being hit by the Iranian sanctions—we must realize that there is a limit to what is bearable in terms of the national interest of Germany. There *is* a reaction. Sanctions are not a good thing. This is not the way to conduct policy. Iran must be integrated into a security architecture. If you isolate a country, if you demonize it, and if you take a one-sided view from Israel and Saudi Arabia, as unfortunately President Trump seems to be doing, this can become a prescription for disaster.

I think sanctions are not working. Look at Russia. Contrary to expectations, Russia has made it clear that it will never change its position on Crimea. The actual situation in Crimea has nothing to do with the narrative spun in the West. The dynamic is quite different: It all started with the policy of regime change. You have to look at the Project for a New American Century, the role of Victoria Nuland, and the EU Association Agreement. You have to look at many factors, in looking at the Crimea. Did Putin change his policy? No.

kremlin.ru

Russia President Vladimir Putin (behind marching soldiers) lays a wreath at the Tomb of the Unknown Soldier on Victory Day, May 9, 2018.

Did it lead to a regime change? No. Putin was just re-elected with a large majority. Sanctions are just not a useful policy tool.

The *only* way you can solve any problem in today's world is through diplomacy and negotiations; that's the only way. Any other way—coups, military strikes, regime change, color revolution—all of these are just different degrees of warfare, none of which will result in anything good.

Schlanger: That brings us to the obvious question: We know the Saudis and the Israelis wanted this decision from President Trump. Ultimately, who benefits from these sanctions, these proxy wars, and the overall increase in tension in the world? Who's benefitting from this?

Zepp-LaRouche: Well—the only ones who benefit are those who believe in geopolitics, divide and conquer, that you always have to ally with the weaker against the stronger. The British Empire is famous for having conducted such policy. Netanyahu claims that Iran violated the treaty, but this was not confirmed by the International Atomic Energy Agency. It was rejected by various other UN institutions. So, where does it come from? Even Netanyahu had to backtrack, rehashing old accusations going back to the Bush administration. In a certain sense, you could say that the same kind of destabilization is taking place in Trumpgate, which now turns out to be collusion, not by Trump with Russia but by the former heads of the intelligence agencies of the Obama administration with the British government.

The Skripal case came from the same origin as did the fraud of the so-called chemical weapons attack by the Syrian government. This is a continuation of the same effort. Netanyahu is acting as an instrument of these same interests. This is very dangerous. It's very unfortunate that President Trump again and again has been affected by these forces around him.

Let me emphasize: There must be a complete change in attitude. Geopolitics is the stuff of which two world wars were made. Given that we are celebrating the May 9 victory over fascism in Europe today, we should really make a solemn commitment, "Never Again!" We cannot have world wars again! These destabilizations have the potential of spinning out of control. Should there be a military conflict between Israel and Iran—which is not to be excluded at this point—it could indeed spin out of control and lead to the extinction of civilization. So this is not stuff to be played with.

Schlanger: We see something similar in the reaction to President Putin's inauguration address, where he made a very strong commitment to serve his term, to improve the conditions of the Russian people, with an emphasis on science, technology, industry, longer life expectancy, and higher living standards. Yet the Western press is full of nothing but attacks on Putin as the "new czar." We are seeing the same kind of hysteria all over again. President Trump, however, did congratulate Putin on his inauguration.

Do you have any thoughts on Putin's inauguration

How Many Needless Deaths?   7

and also the Victory Day celebration in Moscow today?

Zepp-LaRouche: President Putin has a clear perspective for the next six years. He has a very ambitious program to improve living standards, longevity, pensions, and many other aspects of life for the Russian people. We will have to wait to see who is appointed to the cabinet and who gets what position, and to see if some of counterproductive liberal policies of the past are unfortunately continued.

There is certainly a big difference between the cynical, almost hysterical reactions in the West, and the way the Chinese responded to Putin's new six-year term in office. The Chinese *Global Times* had a very accurate observation: The relationship between Russia and the West will not improve easily or any time soon, simply because the West is not reconciled to the fact that Russia, under President Putin, has achieved a new power status in the world as a global player, as a country with a vast territory and incredibly vast resources.

I remember very well that many years ago, Madeleine Albright, and also Joschka Fischer, the Greenie foreign minister of Germany, both outrageously claimed that Russia had too many raw materials and that the Russian government therefore cannot be allowed sole access to the use and control of Russian raw materials. This is really the deeper, underlying reason why certain people in the West are so completely freaked out that Putin, in very difficult circumstances, was able to undo what was done to Russia in the Yeltsin period, in which Russia's population collapsed at the rate of 1 million a year.

Putin has restarted the

Xinhua/Ju Peng

China President Xi Jinping (right) holding talks with Kim Jong Un, leader of the Democratic People's Republic of Korea, in China, May 7-8.

Russian economy to a very large extent. He has consolidated a strategic partnership with China. And, despite obvious economic difficulties—resulting from the economic sanctions and various other problems—he has been able to outflank the military containment of Russia, as made public in his March 1 announcement, with the production and deployment of four new weapons systems that render the American anti-ballistic missile system aimed at Russia obsolete.

Putin has said that Russia is still facing a period of great challenges. He has, in my opinion, managed to do quite an enormous job: All the demonization against him is because he did that. Russia was supposed to continue in the path set by Yeltsin: Submit to the West, to liberal policies, and to shock therapy. Russia has now resumed its status as a world power, to the chagrin of the geopoliticians in the West.

Schlanger: The geopoliticians in the West are screaming about China also. As you have pointed out in the last couple of days, there have been tremendous advances in diplomatic activity in Asia: the follow-up meeting of North Korean leader Kim with President Xi of China, and announcements of North Korea being brought into the Belt and Road Initiative, following the Kim meeting with President Moon Jae-in of South Korea. This is all very promising.

What can you tell us about these developments?

Zepp-LaRouche: Hopefully, the cancellation of the Iran deal will not affect this, which I'm quite worried about.

When Kim Jong-un and Moon Jae-in met, President Moon gave his North Korean

Xinhua/Korean Central News Agency

U.S. Secretary of State Mike Pompeo (left) shaking hands with Kim Jong Un, top leader of the Democreatic People's Republic of Korea, May 9, 2018.

counterpart a thumb drive with a whole development plan for North Korea, involving three economic corridors—railway lines connecting all the way from South Korea through North Korea to China, and to the Trans-Siberian Railway. There are extensive discussions in Moscow about the Tumen River Project. This is a fantastic economic development plan that involves Russia, China, and North Korea. It has the potential to make this region, which is now very underdeveloped, into a big transport hub for all of Asia.

If this program continues to move ahead, we will be seeing an economic miracle between the two Koreas, paving the way for peaceful unification and integration into the Belt and Road Initiative, transforming this area of the world from a crisis spot into one of its most prosperous regions. The fact that Trump's new Secretary of State, Mike Pompeo, was just again in North Korea, preparing the summit between Trump and Kim, means, as of now, it's still on a very good track.

This development clearly demonstrates that if political leaders approach such problems with good will, you can take any crisis—*any* crisis—and solve it exactly the way this was solved. There were extensive back-channel discussions involving Russia, China, and the United States. The Korean developments are a very powerful example, showing that with good will, you can turn the worst crisis into its opposite and make it a hopeful perspective. So I really hope this lesson is truly learned. The same method can and should be applied to Southwest Asia right now. The fact that the New Silk Road is the most dynamic development on the planet, should encourage everyone to see the benefit of cooperating and joining in.

Schlanger: On that latter point, the dynamic development of the New Silk Road, new figures have just been released that highlight the point you've been making about the U.S. deficit in its trade with China. As the Silk Road project expands and grows, China is *importing more*. These figures show a massive increase in trade, and interestingly, China is importing almost as much as it is exporting: So perhaps this lesson will be learned by people in the United States.

Helga, I wonder if you have some thoughts on the meetings now taking place between China, South Korea, and Japan. That's another part of this picture.

Zepp-LaRouche: Yes. The summit meeting of the leaders of these three countries is happening today. That is extremely important, given the recent strategic

North Korea, Russia to push ahead with new bridge on Tumen River

DPRK minister says project could improve trade and economic relations

Dagyum Ji

realignment of Japan, in which Prime Minister Shinzo Abe is now openly cooperating with the Belt and Road Initiative. South Korea is offering to mediate between North Korea and Japan to facilitate North Korean leader Kim Jong-un's expressed desire to have a summit with Prime Minister Abe. All of this is really hopeful, and is going in the right direction.

The Belt and Road trade figures you mentioned are quite relevant. The Chinese government issued statistics for 2017 showing that all the propaganda about how all the countries trading with China have been drawn into a debt trap is completely ridiculous. The total dollar value of the trade between China and 71 countries of the Belt and Road Initiative was $1.5 trillion in 2017. About $666 billion of that trade was China importing from these countries. Exports from China were about $750 billion. The dollar value of imports grew by 20%, while exports grew by 8.5%. So it's almost a balanced trade picture.

This shows that the accusation that China is just exerting its influence to the disadvantage of the participating countries is absolutely not true. These countries have been economically invigorated and are exporting to many other countries in addition to China. It is a complete success story. This is where real growth in the world's economy is taking place.

Schlanger: Instead of reflecting that reality, most of

the discussion in the West is about the so-called "China debt bubble," the "Belt and Road debt bubble," when in fact, it's the debt bubble in the West which threatens the world economy.

I know you looked at Nomi Prins' new book. There's a lot more material coming out. It's ironic that the people who scream about China's debt—when that is *debt as credit* going into real physical production—have nothing to say about the unsustainable volume of debt that continues to grow in the West. Highly incongruous, isn't it?

Zepp-LaRouche: It's not only incongruous: it's reckless. Dangers exist such as the possibility of Southwest Asia spinning out of control, or other such security dangers. The other major danger is the uncontrolled blowout of the trans-Atlantic financial system. On her book tour, Nomi Prins is emphasizing again and again, that all the parameters of the financial crisis are 40% worse than in 2008. Her book is notably titled *Collu$ion: How the Central Bankers Rigged the World*—so she's writing about quite a different form of collusion.

This *is* the unspoken danger, and the only way that danger can be eliminated is with the full Four Laws package designed by my husband, Lyndon LaRouche, in 2014. We need those key measures: Glass-Steagall in the tradition of Franklin Roosevelt, Hamiltonian banking as in Hamilton's National Bank; a credit system; and most importantly, given the collapse of productivity in Western economies due to the toxic mix of opium addiction, desperation, depression, Greenie ideology, and destructive monetarist policies, a crash science-driver program to increase the productivity of the economy.

The Western economies overall, despite some bright spots here and there, urgently need a significant boost. The only way to get such a boost in productivity is to insert a qualitative, higher level of energy-flux density into the production process that would include a crash program for the development of controlled thermonuclear fusion power, and international cooperation in space technology and exploration. That is the pathway to reinvigorate and foster innovation throughout the entire economy.

That requires a completely New Paradigm in relations among nations, all working together in the Belt and Road Initiative, the New Silk Road, in joint ventures in third countries, development of the Middle East together, and development of Africa and Latin America. We really have to fight for our future, and not stay in the prejudices of the old paradigm. Because if enough of us don't join that fight, I don't think the chances for mankind to make it are very high.

If President Trump were to stick to his election promises, and promises he made many times afterwards in rallies, to implement Glass-Steagall, and to go back to the American System of economy, cooperation with China would be very easy. The American System is much, much closer to the Chinese model than most people realize, because it is based on state intervention, that certain areas of the economy are the task of the state, not of private industry. It's no coincidence that Benjamin Franklin was a follower of Confucius and that Sun Yat-sen was inspired by the American System. There are many, many parallels and connections, which would actually make cooperation very easy.

Remember that Wall Street and the City of London, even more so if that's possible, remain totally dead set against those principles and their practical application in U.S.-Chinese cooperation. We clearly need an international mobilization to implement Glass-Steagall before the crash comes. Because, should the crash come without such banking re-regulation in place and progress being made in getting rid of the speculative bubble, the danger is of a plunge into chaos that would almost certainly be a trigger for war.

So I urge you: Join the Schiller Institute. Help us in this mobilization to make the alternative of the New Silk Road as a New Paradigm more known. Once people know about the dynamic, rapidly growing New Silk Road developments, they get a completely different idea of what is possible. Solutions to the crises of today's world are available but more people must mobilize—these solutions don't come on their own.

Schlanger: I think that's a fitting way to close our discussion on this Victory Day. One can learn the lessons of the past, but it requires critical thinking. The Schiller Institute website has numerous articles by Helga Zepp-LaRouche as well as presentations she's given on the lessons of the 20th Century and the danger of sleep-walking into a new world war.

So Helga, on this Victory Day, I thank you for reiterating these points. Again, I urge you, our viewers, to go to our website and become a member of the Schiller Institute, because we are the one force in the world that is absolutely clear on these issues.

Thank you all for joining us, and thank you, Helga, for being with us today.

China's Lunar Program Is Breaking New Ground

by Marsha Freeman

May 13—A small Chinese satellite, named Queqiao, or "magpie bridge," scheduled for launch on May 21, will play a critical role in the world's first landing of a spacecraft, Chang'e-4, on the far side of the Moon, now planned for the end of 2018. Because there is no line of sight between the Earth and the lunar far side, the Queqiao relay satellite will be placed close to half a million kilometers from Earth, in a gravitationally stable "halo" orbit, at the second Earth-Moon Lagrange Point. It will hover more than 60,000 kilometers from the lunar far side. From there, with a line of sight both to Earth and the lunar far side, it can send data back to Earth that is collected by the Chang'e-4 lander and rover, and at the same time, relay commands from Earth to the spacecraft on the Moon. This complex, two-spacecraft mission will reveal in some detail the hemisphere of the Moon that has only been seen until now in glances, first by the Soviet Luna 3 mission in 1959, and then by Apollo astronauts and later unmanned spacecraft orbiting the Moon.

China National Space Administration

An artist's illustration of a planned communications spacecraft that will relay data between controllers on Earth, and China's Chang'e 4 lander and rover on the Moon's far side.

The naming of the satellite harks back to Chinese mythology. Queqiao refers to the Magpie Bridge myth, which reportedly dates back as far as the Sixth Century B.C. As the story goes, a Weaver Girl and a Cowherd are separated by the Silver River, which represents the Milky Way. The two lovers are only reunited for one day each year, by a bridge formed by the wings of a flock of magpies. Thus this relay satellite will be the bridge between the Earth and Chang'e-4.

The Chinese lunar program is a step-by-step series of progressively more difficult missions. The three-phase Chang'e set began in 2007 by orbiting the Moon. The next goal was to land on the Moon, which Chang'e-3 did successfully in 2013. And the final step will be to return a sample of lunar rocks and soil, likely in 2020.

Landing on the far side was not one of the missions on the original agenda of the three-phase lunar program.

A Mission of 'Firsts'

The Chang'e-4 spacecraft was built as a back-up for the Chang'e-3 lunar lander. The success of that mission meant that it did not have to be repeated, and the lander could be repurposed. The scientists chose a mission, landing on the far side, that had never been done before.

At the same time that China's lunar scientists have broadened the goals of the program to include the far side landing, they have opened up the missions to international cooperation.

Along with its main role as a communications relay, Queqiao will also carry the Netherlands-China Low Frequency Explorer, which will carry out radio astronomy experiments. In December, if all goes well with the relay satellite, Chang'e-4 will be launched. The lander carries a Landing Camera, Terrain Camera, Low Frequency Spectrometer, and Lunar Lander Neutrons and Dosimetry experiment, which were all developed in Germany.

The Chang'e-4 lander will carry out another "first." The probe will carry a "mini-biosphere," bringing an array of biology experiments to the lifeless Moon. Inside a small tin will be potato and arabidopsis seeds, along with silkworm eggs. The experiments were designed by 28 Chinese universities, and it is hoped that as the seedlings grow, they produce the oxygen that the silkworms need. "We want to study the respiration of the seeds and photosynthesis on the Moon," Lui Hanlong from Chongqing University explained.

The Chang'e-4 mission will also carry along secondary payloads that are hitching a ride on the rocket to the Moon. Two microsatellites, each weighing about 90 pounds, will carry out astronomy objectives, as they fly in formation orbiting the Moon. They will observe the sky in the very low frequency range of the electromagnetic spectrum, as a test run for future potential astronomy missions. "Many astronomers around the world had proposed to observe at this low frequency range from space," said Chen Xuelei of the National Astronomical Observatory of China, last month, "and now we are proud that [the] Chang'e-4 mission will give us the opportunity to make the first peek at the heavens in this frequency range."

Students at the Harbin Institute of Technology developed an amateur radio payload for the first microsatellite. The second will carry a microcamera developed by King Abdulaziz City for Science and Technology in Saudi Arabia.

Follow-on lunar missions are now under discussion. One region of the Moon of particular interest is the South Pole. Orbiting spacecraft have indicated caches of water ice at the pole, in ultra-cold regions at the floor of craters which are in perennial darkness. Last year, the deputy director of China's Lunar Exploration and Space Program Center, Pei Zhaoyu, reported that China

Far side of the Moon.

NASA Goddard Space Flight Center Scientific Visualization Studio

"will carry out three missions at the Moon's polar regions, to research the geological structure and mineral composition of its South Pole, and we will take samples back from the Moon on one of these missions."

The South Pole-Aitken Basin could well be a target.

Why the Far Side?

Just comparing photographs of the near and far sides of the Moon demonstrates why exploration of the 40% of the Moon's surface that never faces the Earth will help provide answers to questions such as the formation, evolution, and development of the Solar System. The dominating feature on the far side is the South Pole-Aitken Basin. It is the oldest extant feature on the Moon, and one of the largest impact basins in the Solar System. The far-side geology lacks the smooth *maria* characteristic of near-side volcanic eruptions, which has been taken to indicate that the surface is older, formed before there was volcanic activity. But just recently, scientists have suggested that volcanic eruptions took place more recently than previously understood, millions rather than billions of years ago. Taking *in situ* measurements may help to refine further the various geologic ages of the Moon.

Analysis of rocks in the Basin using photographs taken from orbit, suggests that the rocks are unique. The crater is so deep—at about 6 kilometers—that the rocks would likely be older and of a different composition than those that have been sampled on the near side in the past, by Apollo astronauts and Russian robots. Such sample analysis will shed light on an age still present on the Moon, which history has virtually disappeared from the geologically active Earth.

Shielded from the electromagnetically noisy Earth, by facing away from the Earth, the far side of the Moon presents a unique opportunity to open a window to a portion of the electromagnetic spectrum otherwise hidden from view. Since the early days of lunar exploration, scientists have been anxious to put a radio telescope on the far side, to "look" out at the universe in very low frequencies. A broad array of phenomena could become visible, including those that are well known, but will look "new" in a different wavelength, such as the imaging of planets and the detection of asteroids, comets, and radio-emitting galaxies.

There has been conjecture that the future fuel for fusion energy—helium-3—that is deposited in the lunar soil by the solar wind, may be more "concentrated" on the far side than on the Earth-facing side (although "concentration" is relative, since the amount is in parts per billion). It may be that the side of the Moon facing the Earth is partially shielded from the Sun, which lowers the rate of deposition of the helium-3. Determining whether there is a difference will be one of the most interesting findings of the mission.

While China is in final testing for the launch of the Chang'e-4 to the far side, it is also readying the Chang'e-5 sample return mission. The date of that launch will be determined by the readiness of the Long March 5 rocket. This four-craft mission needs the larger Long March 5 launcher, which suffered an accident last July.

The sample return mission will set four new records in the Chinese lunar program. The lander will automatically collect samples of lunar dust and soil. It will place them in a hermetically sealed capsule. The capsule will automatically blast off from the surface of the Moon, and rendezvous and dock with a craft in orbit. As it approaches Earth, the capsule will undock from the or-

biter and come back to Earth, at an interplanetary high velocity. Due to the complexity of the mission, as with automated sample returns in the past, the samples will be taken from a near-equatorial region on the lunar near side, where the craft are able to communicate directly with Earth.

Scientists are now planning a fourth phase of the Chinese lunar program, which will consist of three or four missions, between 2020 and 2030. The aim is to start to use the resources on the Moon. The chief designer of the Chang'e program, Wu Weiren, told China Central Television in March, that the South Pole would be a key target for a robotic research station. "As only the Moon's South Pole can receive sunlight in most of its area throughout the year, we want to land at such a place where there might be abundant sunshine and possibly water to build a research station to carry out relevant research using resources there," he explained. "Nobody has ever landed there yet. So it will be the first landing if we make it."

Chinese scientists have been awaiting a decision by the government to proceed with the most challenging mission of all—a manned landing on the Moon. During the national Space Day celebrations on April 24, the chief designer of China's manned space program, Zhou Jianping, hinted: "We have had in-depth discussions with many experts about manned lunar exploration, and conducted research on key technologies in recent years." Chinese scientists have started soliciting proposals for manned lunar landing and ascent vehicles from the public.

After the completion of this first three-phase lunar exploration program with the Chang'e-5 sample return, China will be resuming its manned space missions, as it begins assembly of a manned space station about two years from now. In the meantime, China is engaged in a broadening array of science, technology, and engineering projects.

Beijing to New York in Two Hours

Wind tunnel tests are underway in China on a novel hypersonic airplane design. The tests have reached speeds of Mach 7, or 5,600 miles per hour. This is one of a number of projects underway, including rocket-powered reusable space planes and scramjet engines, to demonstrate next-generation vehicles that are reusable and fast, with both military and civilian applications. As Russian President Putin stated on March 1, when describing the advanced weapons systems under

How Many Needless Deaths?   13

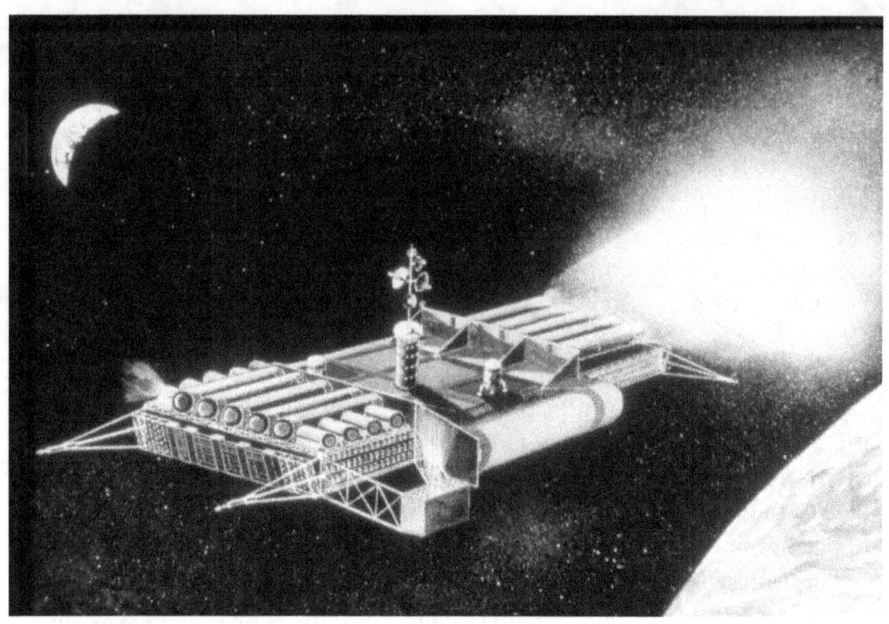

Krafft Ehricke's painting of a proposed nuclear space freighter that he designed.

and Technology Corporation that the space plane will be flight-tested in 2020, as one milestone on a long-term space transportation road map released at the end of last year. Covering a period up to 2040, the road map includes the Saturn V-class heavy lift Long March 9, and fully reusable launch vehicles by 2035.

Most interesting is the brief mention of a nuclear-powered space shuttle, to be operational in 2040. By that time, lunar settlements, mining, and industrial facilities will have transportation requirements that the late space visionary, Krafft Ehricke, proposed would require nuclear freighters, cycling between lunar and Earth orbit. The road map describes the nuclear shuttle as able to support large-scale exploration and the development of space resources such as the mining of asteroids.

Spurring Innovation

Over the past year, China's aerospace industry has begun to move to enlist the energies of private companies and individuals in space technology. New companies, often spun off from established institutions, are producing rocket engines and rockets, vehicles for space tourists, and microsatellites, with the aim of introducing more innovative technology into the economy, especially in the fields of robotics, aviation, and astronautics. Although there are perhaps only a dozen aerospace companies raising capital in China, with encouragement from state institutions—both technical and financial—it is a sector that is going to grow.

China's President Xi Jinping has made investment in science and technology—to spur innovation and drive economic growth—a hallmark of his presidency. As China eliminates the last vestiges of poverty, the up-shift in the population's standard of living and access to education will enable increases in productivity, as China becomes a "knowledge-based economy."

This process will increase the free energy available for pushing further into the frontiers of science and technology.

development in Russia, such speed gives the vehicle a global reach, and nullifies any ballistic missile defense system. And while U.S. military officials expressed shock at the Russian developments, in fact, the United States, China, and Russia have been investigating hypersonic ramjet and scramjet technologies for decades. At the Key Laboratory of High Temperature Gas Dynamics, a record-breaking wind tunnel to obtain speeds of Mach 36 (more than 30,000 miles per hour) is being designed, to put China at the forefront of hypersonic research. For reference, an aircraft at that speed would be able to fly from China to California in 14 minutes. It would also be capable of transporting people and payloads to orbit.

The wind tunnels are also being used to test designs for reusable space planes. The space plane would be able to take off horizontally from an airport, and return to Earth after having delivered cargo and people to orbit. It is being designed with the potential to take tourists to space, launch satellites, deliver supplies to the space station, and carry out emergency space rescue missions. Unlike the U.S. Space Shuttle, the Chinese model will not use rocket engines to obtain the speed required for orbit, but will switch to ramjet propulsion once high in the atmosphere. Chinese projections indicate that the cost of launch to low Earth orbit could be reduced to one tenth the cost of expendable rockets.

It has been reported by China Aerospace Science

Return of Malaysian Prime Minister Mahathir Reflects World Paradigm Change

by Michael O. Billington

May 10—Dr. Mahathir Mohamad was once again sworn in as the next Prime Minister of Malaysia today, following the stunning and overwhelming victory by the opposition coalition he put together to challenge his former UMNO party and his former protégé, Najib Razak, in the May 9 election. This is the first time since independence from the British in 1957 that the UMNO coalition has been removed from government.

Dr. Mahathir, now 92 years old, served as Prime Minister from 1981 to 2003,

Mahathir Mohamad on his Twitter page.

and famously stood up to George Soros and the IMF in the 1997-98 "Asia Crisis," rejecting IMF dictates to impose austerity, and instead imposing capital controls on the national currency, the ringgit, and declaring currency speculation by Soros and his fellow vultures to be "unnecessary, unproductive and immoral." He also fired his Deputy, Anwar Ibrahim, who had backed the IMF and Soros against Mahathir. At the time, *EIR*'s many reports on the global financial crisis and on the crimes of George Soros were being followed closely within the Malaysian government, while *EIR* took it upon itself to circulate Mahathir's speeches and articles around the world, where other leaders suffering from "IMF conditionalities" were grateful readers.

Mahathir had been the longest serving Prime Minister of Malaysia, voluntarily stepping down in 2003. In 2015, however, he launched a fight against Najib and his own party over declining economic growth and corruption, which peaked with the "One Malaysia Development Berhad" (1MDB) scandal, a multi-billion dollar investment fund set up by Najib. Nearly $700 million went missing from 1MDB and showed up in accounts connected to Najib, while billions more are still unaccounted for. The case is under investigation in the United States and Singapore, but Najib quashed any serious investigation within Malaysia.

Mahathir formed his own party, joined a coalition (Pakatan Harapan, Alliance of Hope) that included several of his former enemies and, to the shock of most experts, has now won the national election.

Mahathir and the Belt and Road

In his press conference Thursday morning, the first question was about China and his view of the Belt and Road Initiative. During the campaign, Mahathir had been highly critical of several deals struck with China by Prime Minister Najib, because of what Mahathir considered to be conditions unfavorable to Malaysia. Answering at length, Mahathir made clear that he fully supports the Belt and Road, and will work closely with China, while also wanting to review some of the contracts. His answer:

We need to study all the things done by the previous government, not only about China—a lot of things inside the country. China has a long experience dealing with unequal treaties [under the British —ed.], and China renegotiated them. So if necessary we will renegotiate the terms. But

Dr. Mahathir Mohamad on May 10, the first day on the job after his election.

Mahathir's facebook page

what amount of money was borrowed by the government? [Malaysian ringgit] 55 billion [$14 billion] for the East-West railroad, and lots of other things which will be a great burden on the government. The government must try to reduce borrowing, otherwise we will be in bad shape.

As far as the Belt and Road problem—we have no problem with that. Except we don't want to see warships in the region, because warships attract other warships, and things will become tense. In the past we had a nuclear free zone, so we would not like to have potential warfare in this country.

But we support the Belt and Road program. In fact, I myself wrote to Xi Jinping on the need of a land connection with Europe using trains, which are faster than ships. When the demand for oil grew, ships were built bigger and bigger, reaching a half million tons, but trains remained small, not long enough. So I suggested to Xi Jinping in a personal letter that we need big trains, and China has the technology to build big trains, to take goods to Europe, and also to make Central Asia— Kazakhstan, Uzbekistan, and so on—to be more accessible, to transfer their goods, their raw materials, to China, to Japan, and to Southeast Asia.

That is our policy.

Global Implications

Like the Brexit vote, the election of Rodrigo Duterte to the Presidency of the Philippines, and the election of Donald Trump to the Presidency of the United States, the return to leadership of Dr. Mahathir Mohamad expresses the unfolding change in the global paradigm, with a great potential to help resolve many crises in Southwest Asia and elsewhere in the developing world.

One businessman who has worked on international projects with Mahathir's leading economic advisor, Daim Zainudden—who will serve on Mahathir's Council of Elders to get the new administration up and running—told *EIR* after the election that he has seen evidence that Mahathir still enjoys huge respect around the world, especially in the majority Islamic nations, for his defense of development and sovereignty.

The financial oligarchy in the West is wary of Mahathir's return to power. Back in 1997, after Soros and his ilk had unleashed the attack on the Asian currencies— which Lyndon LaRouche identified at the time as the first blow of a global financial breakdown—Mahathir identified Soros and the appropriately named "vulture funds" for their crimes. On Sept. 19, 1997, the day before Mahathir was to speak at an IMF meeting in Hong Kong, the *Wall Street Journal*'s Asian edition ran a front page freakout: "Malaysia's Mahathir Finds Strange Source for Soros Campaign: Asian Country's Media Tap U.S. Conspiracy Theorist Lyndon LaRouche, Jr." Complaining that *EIR*'s April 1997 report, *The True Story of Soros the Golem—A Profile of Mega-Speculator George Soros*, was widely circulating in Malaysia, the *Journal* wrote:

Mr. LaRouche has long been at odds with the U.S. political mainstream, which regards him as an extremist in his views about reforming the global financial system. But his theories receive a warmer reception in Malaysia, where the 60-page *EIR* report on Mr. Soros has been passed among Malaysian editors, intellectuals and politicians.

Mahathir has always been a major thorn in the side of the British and others in the West who have tried, and are still trying, to divide Asia into pro- and anti-China blocs, to maintain the British Empire's division between East and West. In an interview with this author for *EIR* on Feb. 16, 2014, Dr. Mahathir commented on his meeting with President Xi Jinping in Kuala Lumpur soon after Xi had announced the Maritime Silk Road in Indonesia, in October 2013. Mahathir and Xi created a new institution, the Cheng Ho Association, named after Adm. Cheng Ho (Zheng He), who led the huge armada of Chinese Treasure Ships to the West in the 15th Century. Mahathir said:

Kassim of Bernama

Mahathir (left) meeting with the author's wife, Gail Billington, on Jan. 22, 1999, in Kuala Lumpur, Malaysia.

[Cheng Ho] is a remarkable leader, a remarkable man. He came with very powerful forces, not to conquer, but to establish diplomatic relations with countries. China never attempted to conquer countries. They wanted to establish diplomatic relations and trade with these countries. This contrasts with the first Portuguese—with Vasco da Gama, Afonso de Albuquerque, and Diogo Lopes de Sequeira—all of whom came here in order to conquer. The Portuguese arrived in Malacca in 1509. Two years later, they conquered Malacca. The Chinese had been in Malacca for many, many years before that, and never conquered Malacca, although they had so many Chinese in this country who could have formed a fifth-column for them. But they never tried to conquer. So there is this difference between Cheng Ho and the Portuguese and the other Europeans. Cheng Ho established friendships. So this Association that we are going to form is in order to celebrate friendship between nations. There will be an award for the people who work most to bring about friendship between countries.

Asked about terrorism and the violent divisions within the Islamic world, Mahathir answered: "At the back of this all is the British. The British have caused more damage in this world than anybody else, through their colonial policies in the past, and through the conclusion of their decolonization process—all these things have left behind a legacy that leads to war."

Mahathir and LaRouche

As the *Wall Street Journal* painfully noted, Mahathir and his circle had been following LaRouche's unique analysis of world affairs, and his visionary economic and development proposals for several years when the 1997 Asian crisis erupted. Western specula-

George Nathaniel Lord Curzon, Viceroy of India. In EIR*'s warning to the "Asian Tigers" that they were being set up with hot money,* EIR *ran this photo with the caption: "This is how the British treat tigers."*

How Many Needless Deaths?   17

tors had been massively pumping hot money into what they called the "Asian Tiger" economies and the emerging Southeast Asian economies, including Thailand, Indonesia, and Malaysia. The dumb pundits were universally assuring these countries that the bonanzas in the speculative markets would go on forever. One exception was LaRouche's *EIR*. The Feb. 7, 1997 issue of *EIR* carried an article by Michael and Gail Billington titled, "London Sells a Killer 'Tiger' Tonic to Southeast Asia," and a national *EIR* conference that month featured a presentation by Gail Billington on the same theme—that the Asian Tigers were about to "head down Mexico way," referring to the collapse of the Mexican currency and economy in 1994. The photograph accompanying the article showed a team of British oligarchs, kneeling with their rifles over a dead tiger after a hunting party in the colonies.

Dr. Mahathir expressed his gratitude for *EIR*'s role in a letter of condolence upon Gail Billington's death in 2012:

> My condolences on the passing away of Gail. Gail's demise is a loss not only to you, but to all who believe in truth and justice in the perception of the affairs of the world. Gail did much to correct the wrong image of Malaysia created by the controlled Western Press, especially during the financial crisis of East Asia. I pray to God that He will grant Gail rest in peace.
>
> Signed, Dr. Mahathir bin Mohamad, Former Prime Minister of Malaysia.

Anwar Ibrahim's Role

As mentioned, Dr. Mahathir fired his deputy, Anwar Ibrahim, at the time of the 1997 crisis. Apart from his backing of IMF demands, Anwar had a history of ties to the Muslim Brotherhood and Saudi Arabia. Following his dismissal and subsequent arrest on charges of sodomy, Anwar became the darling of the Western neocons and financial oligarchs, including Soros, Al Gore, and Paul Wolfowitz, in a campaign to demonize Mahathir and organize a "color revolution" to bring down his government.

swiss-image.ch/Michael Wuertenberg
Defeated former Prime Minister Najib Razak. His investment fund 1MBD went missing several billion dollars, which will now be thoroughly investigated.

This author confronted Anwar in person and in print on his role on behalf of the British.

Ironically, Mahathir dropped his enmity to Anwar, and others of Anwar's circle in Malaysia, when he recognized that the massive corruption of the Najib government required it. Mahathir joined in a coalition with Anwar's People's Justice Party, currently run by Anwar's wife, Wan Azizah Wan Ismail, while Anwar is serving a second sentence for sodomy. Mahathir has even pledged to pardon Anwar and restore his rights to participate in politics. In fact, he has stated that he only plans to serve as Prime Minister for two years or less, and that Anwar could then be available to run for leadership of the coalition.

Those close to Mahathir believe that Anwar is capable of change, and that in any case, Mahathir and his close associates will have time to install a competent team in the key positions, to restore Malaysia to its place as a model for development internationally, as it was under Mahathir's earlier leadership.

One close associate who works in development projects internationally, told *EIR* that Mahathir is still greatly admired around the world, especially in the Islamic nations. His return to office, and his critical role in promoting the spirit of the new Silk Road, can and must be brought to bear in solving other crisis spots, and emphatically those in Southwest Asia, on the basis of development and the common aims of Mankind.

Firdaus Latif
Anwar Ibrahim. Will he continue taking orders from the neocons and vulture funds, or can he change?

Accelerating 'Win-Win' Good Will Between China and the United States

by Robert L. Baker

May 12—On May 3 in Des Moines, Iowa, a new book, *'Old Friends': The Xi Jinping—Iowa Story*, was released with full diplomatic honors at a reception attended by about 200. The author, Sarah Lande of Muscatine, Iowa, came to know Xi Jinping, now President of China, back in 1985, when he first visited Des Moines while leading an agriculture tour of the region. Lande met him again several times, including when, as Vice-President, Xi returned to Muscatine in 2012. In June that same year, Lande visited China, and met Xi's wife, Peng Liyuan.

From 1988 to 1998, Lande served as the first Executive Director for Iowa Sister States, a state-supported non-profit organization that builds Iowa's cultural, economic, and educational partnerships

"Old Friends": The Xi Jinping - Iowa Story

"老朋友":习近平与艾奥瓦的故事

Compiled and told by Sarah D. Lande

萨拉·兰蒂讲述编写

Schiller Institute/Robert Baker

Sarah Lande (right) discussing her new book, shown here with Daniel Stein, Chairman of the Muscatine China Initiatives Committee.

Schiller Institute/Robert Baker

Participants listening to Lande's presentation. Pictures in the background are by Mr. Bai Runzhang, Vice-Chairman of the Standing Committee of the Tenth People's Congress, Hebei Province, China.

Schiller Institute/Robert Baker

Sarah Lande being interviewed at the Des Moines event by Wang Ping of the Xinhua News Agency.

Schiller Institute/Robert Baker

Former mayor of Muscatine, DeWayne Hopkins, and his wife Jill (left). From right, Albert Liu, who guided the language translations in Sarah Lande's book, Dan Stein, and Mr. Bai Runzhang, who was with Xi Jinping when he first came to Iowa in 1985.

Schiller Institute/Robert Baker

Classical musicians playing Beethoven, as people gathered before Sarah Lande's book release at the historic World Food Prize Building in Des Moines, Iowa.

with the world, including Hebei Province in northern China, with which Iowa established a sister-state agreement in 1983. Members have pride in their state of Iowa and wish to share with the world their special bond of friendship with President of China Xi Jinping and how their friendship has grown. Sarah Lande was awarded the title of Honorary Friendship Ambassador in 2013 by the Chinese People's Association for Friendship with Foreign Countries. It is believed Lande's book will be published in China within this year.

The new book is bilingual (English and Chinese) and includes photographs personally selected by Xi specifically for the project. Lande said that she hopes the book's stories will "inspire U.S.-China relations and inspire citizen ambassadors of any age, long into the future."

The foreword to the book was written by the current United States Ambassador to China, Terry Branstad, former Governor of Iowa (1988-1999, and 2011-2017), who met and hosted Xi on his visit in 2012. Branstad writes about the "significance of citizen diplomacy" and how it is demonstrated by the "remarkable story of President Xi Jinping" and the exchanges with Iowa. Xi, himself, contributed these words: "Our memoir, 'The Xi Jinping—Iowa Story,' will share our special story of friendship with the world. And I say, today we celebrate with you.... So this is truly a memoir of the people, by the people, and for the people. It's a wonderful story showing Iowa's people-to-people friendship at its finest."

In addition to the author, speakers at the May 3 event could be grouped into Old Friends, Iowa Friends, and China Friends. Old Friends included Mr. Bai Runzhang, one of the five-person Chinese agricultural delegation led by Xi that visited Iowa in 1985, when Xi was an official in Hebei Province; Kenneth Quinn, former United States Ambassador to Cambodia and currently President of the World Food Prize Foundation; and Dan Stein, Chair of the Muscatine China Initiatives Committee.

China Friends included Chinese Ambassador to the United States Cui Tiankai, who emphasized friendship, saying, "The Xi Jinping—Iowa story is a miniature of the past forty years of robust and all-round development of China—U.S. relation, which has served the interests of our two peoples." Also speaking were Mr. Xie Yuan, Vice President of Chinese Peoples Association for Friendship with Foreign Countries; and Mr. Hong Lei, Consul General of the Peoples Republic of China in Chicago.

Greetings from Iowa Friends began with remarks by United States Ambassador to China, Terry Branstad, read by his son Marcus Branstad, and by Iowa Governor Kim Reynolds, read by Paul Pate, Iowa Secretary of State. Former Governor Robert D. Ray's "Special Relationship" was read by David Oman and Ms. Debi Durham, Director of the Iowa Economic Development Authority.

A large contingent of citizens from Muscatine came to Des Moines for the book release. The town is on the Mississippi River, and many recalled how Xi relished a boat ride on the Mississippi, telling Lande and others that he had read Mark Twain, and always wanted to try "life on the Mississippi." Twain is a well-known folk figure in China.

Schiller Institute

From left, Mr. Bai Runzhang and his wife, former mayor DeWayne Hopkins, and Robert Baker.

The book event was held in the Hall of Laureates of the imposing premises of the World Food Prize building, an awards program initiated by the famous crop scientist from Iowa, Dr. Norman Borlaug, known as "father of the Green Revolution." Attendee Robert Baker, of the Schiller Institute, noted the importance of this venue for "win-win" international economic relations. In the Hall is a prominent statue of another famous Iowan, Henry A. Wallace, former Secretary of Agriculture, Secretary of Commerce, and Vice President under Franklin D. Roosevelt, whom Borlaug, in his biography, credits as the original father of the Green Revolution.

The event included a musical offering by the Muscatine High School choral group, sung in Chinese. The song, "Lasting Memory," was composed at the instigation of China's First Lady, Peng Liyuan, for the 30th anniversary celebration in 2013 of Iowa and Hebei Province being sister states. The pre-meeting foyer music was a violin-viola duet playing Bach.

A special reception and exhibit was held the following evening in Muscatine, at the Merrill Hotel and Conference Center, a newly opened luxurious Mississippi riverside boutique hotel, which caters especially to Chinese tourists. Again, the reception was in honor

Invitation to a reception in honor of Mr. Runzhang's donation of his beautiful photos of Chinese agriculture to the Merrill Hotel and the citizens of Muscatine.

Sarah Lande's new book, and the exhibition featured many enlarged photographs of Chinese agricultural vistas by Chinese master photographer, Bai Runzhang, who was also with Xi in the 1985 visit to Muscatine. Titled "Embracing the Land," the exhibit was donated by Mr. Runzhang as a permanent display for the citizens of Iowa. A greeting from China was read by De-Wayne Hopkins, the former Mayor of Muscatine, who hosted then Vice President Xi on a return visit to Iowa. Last July, Hopkins delivered the welcoming speech at a New York City conference titled, "Food for Peace & Thought," co-sponsored by the Schiller Institute, which was attended by a large delegation of Chinese agriculture specialists.

Sarah Lande's book, *'Old Friends': The Xi Jinping—Iowa Story*, is an excellent book to promote, encourage, and represent how people of the United States and China, indeed all nations, can become "Old Friends."

The book can be ordered online at https://www.xijinpingiowamemoir.com/ or Community Foundation of Greater Muscatine https://www.muscatinecommunityfoundation.org/iowa-story-book/ The price of the book is: $50 per book, plus S&H $21 per book.

Shipping is only available within the United States, at this time. Estimated delivery will be 10-14 days.

For bulk orders of 25 or more, please call 563-264-3863.

THE SCHILLER INSTITUTE PRESENTS

A Concert Dedicated to the Spirit of RFK, Beethoven, and the New Paradigm

by John Sigerson

The prospect of ending the senseless, decades-long stalemate between the two Koreas, and of finally bringing the world's two most populous nations, China and India, into a bond of friendship and cooperation based on economic development and the elimination of poverty, cannot but warm the hearts of all men and women of goodwill, pointing a way to a New Paradigm of peaceful relations among nations, based on what uniquely distinguishes man from beast, namely man's creativity and highest purpose to improve and enrich the lives of everyone on (and above) this planet.

This prospect is a vindication of the life of John F. Kennedy, and no less of his brother Robert, felled by an assassin's bullet five decades ago, on June 6, 1968 in the midst of his campaign to bring to an end the humiliating war in Vietnam.

It is likewise a vindication of the life's work of Schiller Institute founder Helga Zepp-LaRouche and her husband, physical economist Lyndon LaRouche, whose banner of a creativity-based economic policy, replacing the old, fatally flawed money-based model, is now being carried by China, in the form of its worldwide Belt and Road Initiative for the elimination of poverty not just in China, but everywhere.

And Ludwig van Beethoven, who, like all great poets, had his hand firmly planted on the world's pulse, is also now vindicated! Indeed, Beethoven once commented to a friend that if people took seriously the discovered principles embedded in his compositions, warfare within and among nations would become an impossibility. For him, as well as for "Poet of Freedom" Friedrich Schiller, the content and intent of peace is the ennoblement of the human soul, so that the individual can proceed to ennoble others as well. As Beethoven jotted down, while sketching out the "Dona nobis pacem" (Give us peace) section of his mighty *Missa Solemnis*:

> "Stärke der Gesinnungen des innern Friedens über alles ... Sieg!"

> "Strength of sentiments of inner peace above all else ...Victory!"

which he later transformed into the motto of his entire monumental work:

> "Bitte um innern und äussern Frieden."

> "Plea for inner and outward peace."

It is the same with the immortal Schiller: Among his many poems is his "Song of the Bell," in which the joint planning, forging, protection, and raising of the bell is a metaphor for the composition of true political freedom. His poem concludes:

> Come now, with the ropes' whole might,
> From her dungeon swing the bell,
> Till she rise to heaven's height,
> In the realm of sound to dwell!
> Pull and lift—still more!
> See her move and soar!
> Joy unto this city bringing,
> May Peace become her first glad ringing!

The Concert Program

The concert will begin with a selection of African-American Spirituals which is a hallmark of Schiller Institute NYC Chorus's efforts to preserve this precious

Helga Zepp-LaRouche

Schiller Institute New York City Chorus

assertion of man's dignity against all efforts to degrade him to a beast.

The featured work is Beethoven's *Mass in C*, Opus 86, which he composed in 1807 at the behest of Prince Esterházy, son of the late Prince Esterházy who had sponsored Joseph Haydn's career.

Contrary to some who attempt to cast Beethoven as a product of the "Enlightenment," which relegates creativity to the domain of the Unknowable, Beethoven was a true Promethean in the tradition of Plato, Kepler, and Leibniz, and was dedicated to making creative discovery intelligible to all seekers of Truth. He was therefore deeply religious in that sense, i.e., not in the sense of doctrine, and thus his approach to setting the Catholic mass. As he noted in 1818 while working on his *Missa Solemnis*:

> In order to write true church music … look through all the monastic church chorals and also the strophes in the most correct translations and perfect prosody in all Christian-Catholic psalms and hymns generally.
>
> Sacrifice again all the pettinesses of social life to your art. O God above all things! For it is an eternal Providence which directs omnisciently the good and evil fortunes of human men.
>
> Short is the life of man, and whoso bears
> A cruel heart, devising cruel things,
> On him men call down evil from the gods
> While living, and pursue him, when he dies,
> With cruel scoffs. But whoso is of generous
>   heart
> And harbors generous aims, his guests proclaim
> His praises far and wide to all mankind,
> And numberless are they who call him good.
> —Homer
>
> Tranquilly will I submit myself to all vicissitudes and place my sole confidence in Thy unalterable goodness, O God! My soul shall rejoice in Thy immutable servant. Be my rock, my light, forever my trust!

Sad to say, Beethoven's passion for Truth was a bit too much for Prince Esterházy to take. Following the first performance on September 13, 1807, the Prince complained to Countess Henriette Zielinska:

Beethoven's Mass is unbearably ridiculous and detestable, and I am not convinced that it can ever be performed properly. I am angry and mortified.

Nevertheless, two movements of the Mass were joyously received in Vienna the following year, along with his *Choral Fantasy*, Op. 80.

This pairing of the *Mass* and the *Choral Fantasy*, by the way, is significant for Beethoven's creative work in general. Just as his motivic development in his *Mass in C* foreshadows his *Missa Solemnis*, so the main theme of the *Choral Fantasy* points directly to the final choral movement of his *Symphony No. 9*. And it is no accident that the 1824 premiere concert of the *Ninth* also premiered three movements from his *Missa Solemnis*.

The New Paradigm and the Sublime

All great works of Classical art, whether they be music, drama, poetry, the plastic arts, or all combined, are dynamic ideas which impel the beholder into the domain of the Sublime. This is done through stark juxtapositions or paradoxes which are in the domain of metaphor, in the extended sense of William Empson's treatise, *Seven Types of Ambiguity*. (See also Lyndon H. LaRouche, Jr., "On the Subject of Metaphor," *Fidelio*, Vol. 1, No. 3, Fall 1992).

As Schiller writes in his essay, "On the Sublime":

The feeling of the Sublime is a mixed feeling. It is a composite of sorrowfulness, which in its highest gradation is expressed as a shuddering; and of joyfulness, which can intensify into delight, and, although it is not properly pleasure, is what cultured souls prefer by far over all pleasure *per se*. This union of two contradictory sentiments into a single feeling proves our moral self-subsistence in an irrefutable manner.... Through the feeling of the Sublime, therefore, we have the experience that our state of mind is not necessarily governed by the state of our senses: that the laws of nature are not necessarily also our laws, and that we have within us *a self-subsisting principle which is independent of our sense impressions*. [emphasis added]

In the 20th Century, the great conductor Wilhelm Furtwängler put the same principle another way when he argued that actual musical ideas are located entirely outside of sense-perception, "between" or "behind" the notes.

Beethoven's evocation of the Sublime is particularly compelling in the concluding "Agnus Dei" (Lamb of God) movement of both his *Mass in C* and his *Missa Solemnis*. In this section, the wrenching "Agnus Dei, qui tollis peccata mundi" (Lamb of God, who taketh away the sins of the world) assumes a downright warlike cast, as the defenseless Lamb is led to slaughter, only to be interrupted by the gentle, sunny warmth of "Dona nobis pacem," which emerges victorious. And then, just to make the point clear, Beethoven alternates both episodes a second time.

The unifying principle of the Sublime in this concluding movement is reinforced by Beethoven's Motivführung, i.e., his use of inversions and transformations of the very same "rising fourth" thematic material that opens the entire *Mass* in the first "Kyrie" movement.

Brothers (and Sisters)

The audience's moral victory upon contemplation of two brothers locked in seemingly irreconcilable conflict is evident not only in Schiller's famous "Ode to Joy" ("All men become brothers where'er tarries thy gentle wing"), but also in Schiller's very first drama, *The Robbers*, and his penultimate play, *The Bride of Messina*. In the former play, the brothers' dying father, in words laden with Biblical imagery, yet almost Confucian in tone, admonishes:

How lovely a thing it is when brethren dwell together in unity; as the dewdrops of heaven that fall upon the mountains of Zion. Learn to deserve that happiness, young man, and the angels of heaven will sun themselves in thy glory. Let thy wisdom be the wisdom of gray hairs, but let thy heart be the heart of innocent childhood.

Those who know and love Johannes Brahms' *A German Requiem* will immediately recognize "How Lovely Is Thy Dwelling Place."

Such is always the dialog of great artists, across time and space. And such is the substance of the New Paradigm.

The Schiller Institute NYC Chorus presents

DONA NOBIS PACEM: 1968-2018

LUDWIG VAN BEETHOVEN'S

MASS IN C MAJOR

AND AFRICAN-AMERICAN SPIRITUALS

FEATURING

Sarah Abigail Griffiths, *Soprano* · Linda Childs, *Alto*

Greogory Hopkins, *Tenor* · Paul An, *Bass*

John Sigerson, *Conductor*

In 1968, two great American leaders Dr. Martin Luther King Jr., and Robert F. Kennedy were felled by assassins' bullets. On Christmas Eve of the same year, three American astronauts became the first human beings to orbit the moon, demonstrating that the dream of President John F. Kennedy was near realization, even after his untimely death. Now, the American people are called upon to abandon the last half century of degradation and war, and choose the optimistic path, identified as "the future Spirit of Humanity," by Schiller Institute founder Helga Zepp-LaRouche. In that spirit, the genius Ludwig van Beethoven once said that if his music were properly understood, "warfare in and among nations would become an impossibility." This performance is dedicated to that principle, and will be performed at the scientific tuning of C=256Hz.

Sunday, June 10th, 2018, 4:00 p.m.

St. Anthony of Padua Church

155 Sullivan Street, New York, NY

Admission $40 reserved seating, $20 general admission, $10 students and seniors

For tickets, call 646-509-5451 or visit www.bit.ly/pax2018

sinycchorus.com   facebook.com/schillerchorusnyc

Let Us Bury the 'Old, Evil Songs' of a Dying Culture

by Jennifer Pearl and John Sigerson

May 12—The Schiller Boston Community Chorus presented a "Concert for a New Paradigm" on Sunday, May 6, centered on two major works, Robert Schumann's *Dichterliebe*, performed by tenor John Sigerson and pianist Barbara Suhrstedt, and J.S. Bach's choral motet, *Jesu, Meine Freude*. The concert was held at St. Mary's Episcopal Church in Dorchester, Massachusetts

While the concert was sparked by the tragic school shooting in Parkland, Florida earlier this year, it is part of a larger mission by the Schiller Boston chorus to recruit adults and youth, professionals and non-professionals in the city of Boston and surrounding areas to the mission of creating a new American culture to replace the culture of death that has seeped into our republic since the end of World War II.

As Lyndon LaRouche wrote in his 1999 paper, "Star Wars and Littleton," "How does one corrupt innocent children into becoming psychotic-like killers? The quick answer to that question, is: dehumanize the image of man." The violent and degenerate actions of such terrorists groups as ISIS and the American school killers reflect the same quality of dehumanization found in today's movies, music, and popular culture. Combined with the collapsing physical economy of the United States, and the lack of education and productive jobs, this has created a sense of hopelessness among young Americans of all socio-economic backgrounds. While popular music amplifies the current sad state of affairs and comments crudely upon it, it is only through great classical art that you can access the creativity and educate the passionate courage needed to change the current and future condition of mankind.

If America is going to whole-heartedly join the New Silk Road, there has to be a change in our culture. Classical music is currently performed in a boring and literal way to a snooty audience of high-price ticket-holders, while everyone else is watching "The Voice" and rooting for the next teenage pop star. Through our work, we are beginning to demonstrate that the communication of profound ideas through irony is the key to moving the soul of your audience and actually making them better people!

The May 6 concert drew a wide range of people from throughout the Boston area and not the usual "classical music concert-goers." The program began with three African-American spirituals, which set the tone and gave the audience a chance to directly connect, through the English language, to what followed. The spirituals were followed by the aria "Ah la paterna mano," from Giuseppe Verdi's opera *Macbeth*, sung by tenor Brian Landry, and a series of Handel and Brahms songs sung by soprano Annicia Smith and contralto Ana Maria Ugarte.

What Is a Poet To Do?

Central to the program was Robert Schumann's cycle of sixteen songs, *Dichterliebe*, with poetry by Heinrich Heine. John Sigerson prefaced his performance by saying, "This is not a piece about the love affair between two people, but about having

EIRNS/Kevin Pearl

Jennifer Pearl, speaking at "Concert for a New Paradigm" at St. Mary's Episcopal Church in Dorchester, Massachusetts, with Father Edwin Johnson.

a love affair with humanity, and all he or she receives back is a slap in the face. What is a poet to do? The subject of these songs is the poet's struggle with infantile emotions to get through to a higher emotion, represented in the final piece, talking about burying all these old songs."

Properly performed, this song cycle is a frontal assault on the fundamental tenet of Romanticism, namely that since (so the Romantics claim) it is impossible to gain intelligible knowledge of universal principles, all human knowledge must be ultimately based on sense-perception alone, just as it is with other beasts. Locked thus inside the prison of sense-perception, men are simply talking beasts, and can only regulate their affairs through sets of rules governed by logic.

That was the argument of Immanuel Kant (1724-1804), whom the Schiller Institute's namesake, Friedrich Schiller, flatly rejected, and whom Heine directly refuted in his book *Religion and Philosophy in Germany*, aptly describing Kant as "the Robespierre of philosophy" because, rather than chopping off men's heads, Kant wanted to chop off their souls.

As Lyndon LaRouche wrote in 1982 as a commentary on Sigerson's first public performance of *Dichterliebe*:

The *Dichterliebe* is one of the most rip-roaringly funny compositions ever written. An audience which grasps the point will be either doubled over with laughter, or savagely enraged. That is the measure of the proper, successful rendering....

Music's result is exactly the result of poetry, but in terms of a polyphonic domain. That result is irony—is comedy, tragedy, based on the principle of the Socratic dialogue. To this comedy or tragedy only one thing can be added: successful musical (polyphonic) resolution. That latter is the Promethean principle in music. Only Promethean music can be satisfying.

A number of those who attended had never heard live classical music and were visibly awed by the performance of the *Dichterliebe*. Some wondered, how could John remember all those words? One person remarked, "It was so funny, of course—the coffin was so heavy at the end because it had all the loves and losses in it weighing it down."

People were intensely following the English translation of the sixteen-song German cycle. It was so quiet, you could have heard a pin drop in the room, and not one person got up during the entire thirty-minute song cycle. A handful of younger people laughed a lot during the *Dichterliebe*, saying later they "never thought classical music could be so funny!" One leading member of the church commented that he was "with John every step of the way."

Nobody performs this piece, nor other such classical pieces, with this sense of irony. Instead, they are always performed as Romantic, sappy, literal stories that you are supposed to "relate to." But, the relatable aspect of this is not the romanticism but rather the transformation that the artist portrays. This process of transformation, to a higher emotional state and a higher understanding, is the true purpose of art—providing a pathway for the audience to discover things about themselves and the world, such that they might understand better and overcome the problems that they and their world face. We can overcome the problems that prevent us from being better, more creative, and more effective human beings. Such a transformation is a key requirement for the American people to embrace the New Paradigm.

EIRNS/Jennifer Pearl

Soprano Michele Fuchs, performing at "Concert for a New Paradigm" at St. Mary's Episcopal Church in Dorchester, Massachusetts.

EIRNS/Rachel Brown

Tenor John Sigerson and pianist Barbara Suhrstedt, at "Concert for a New Paradigm" at St. Mary's Episcopal Church in Dorchester, Massachusetts.

IT'S NOT THAT EASY TO GET RID OF US

The British Empire Cannot Withstand the Truth

by Ramasimong Phillip Tsokolibane

May 10—Sometime between April 15 and April 20, the website of LaRouche South Africa was attacked by a hacker or hackers, causing it to disappear from the internet entirely. Subsequent investigation has revealed that not only had the website been brought down, but the backup files normally created by the host, which enable a simple restoration of the site, have also been wiped out entirely, as have copies of the same files normally available to the webmaster. Discussions with various specialists in the field confirm that the attack was conducted with a level of sophistication typical of the capability of an intelligence service.

We may never know the identity of the hacker or hackers, but we can state its origin with certainty. We can be certain that this operation was ordered by the highest levels of the British Empire, and carried out by one or more of its numerous assets capable of committing such crimes. Those familiar with the LaRouche movement know that we are the principal enemy of the anti-human, oligarchical cabal that is the British empire. We have insisted that if the world is to survive the present combined economic, financial, and geopolitical crisis, courageous individuals must move their respective governments to make a fundamental break with the

Ramasimong Phillip Tsokolibane

monetarist policies of the British empire which, through its assets, is currently driving the world towards a thermonuclear confrontation with Russia and China. These are the very nations that are leading an emerging New Paradigm, whose origins lie directly in the work over the last half century of the great American economist and statesman, Lyndon LaRouche, and his wife Helga, whose movement I lead in South Africa.

Just prior to the hack of our website, I had delivered written remarks to a conference of the Schiller Institute held in New York City on April 7, in which I called for the creation of a global movement based on Dr. Martin Luther King, Jr.'s principle of creative non-violence, as shared by the father of our nation, Nelson Mandela, in support of the New Paradigm, and against the brutal imperial looting policies of the British Empire and its City of London financial power, including its Wall Street satrapy. My remarks were warmly greeted by those assembled which included representatives from Russia and China, as well as many African nations.

In the days that followed, attacks on the Brutish—and on the outlandish provocations they have authored, including the phony gas attack in Syria they attributed

Former President of South Africa, Jacob Zuma (left) next to the current president, Cyril Ramaphosa. Zuma's speech attacking the role of the British Empire in South Africa was taken offline shortly after it had been posted.

to the Syrian government—became sharper, with Russian Ministry of Foreign Affairs spokeswoman Maria Zakharova's hour-long report on April 19th on the long history of the British Empire's policy of savage brutality. (See item 11, 'Political crimes committed by the UK', on this page: http://www.mid.ru/en/foreign_policy/news/-/asset_publisher/cKNonkJE02Bw/content/id/3178301)

For years, we have urged then President Jacob Zuma to consolidate his turn to the East, towards the New Paradigm based on economic development, by breaking completely with the British Empire. Our website became a source of information supporting this move. It also exposed the British hand behind regime-change efforts in my country. Anyone who wanted to fight the British knew to go to LaRouche South Africa for ammunition and reports on the global fight against the Empire.

Then, on April 21, former President Zuma delivered a one-hour lecture on the crimes of the British Empire in South Africa, at a "Blacks in Dialogue" event in Braamfontein. That video, originally posted at http://www.ann7.com/former-president-jacob-zuma-speaks-of-the-injustices-of-land-dispossession/, has now been deleted, as have all repostings on the Internet. On April 28, I issued a statement in support of Mr. Zuma, adding that this was not an academic matter of historical footnoting,

but the burning issue driving current history. How "convenient" it was that my statement could not be posted, and that our website was not available to those looking to back up Mr. Zuma's history.

And, how convenient it is that our website is down just as our new President, Mr. Cyril Ramaphosa, heads for London to kiss the Royal rump and to present himself in person to take orders from his masters. Adding insult to injury, it has just been announced that the British lawn jockey, former U.S. President Barack Obama, will be delivering the 16th annual Nelson Mandela memorial lecture this July in Johannesburg, on the centenary of our great father's birth. Can you believe that? We had plenty of information on our website demonstrating the disgrace and treacherousness of such a travesty.

The Brutish empire fears the truth, as well it should. But let me state clearly that it shall neither escape the deserved fate of all tyrannies, nor shall its perfidy go unreported, especially here in South Africa. We will shortly bring our website and its truth-telling content back online. We will do our job in bringing about an early defeat and end to the Brutish Empire.

In this, the one hundred year anniversary of the birth of Nelson Mandela, let the truth finally set us free. Patriots: join us in this fight! *Sic transit gloria mundi.*

Zuma Exposes the History of British Imperial Evil in South Africa

May 14—In an hour-long lecture on April 21, South Africa's former President, Jacob Zuma, reviewed the criminality and savagery of the British Empire, as visited upon South Africa in the first hundred years of British conquest. There is no precedent for such an address in South Africa.

For several years, the spokesman for the LaRouche movement in South Africa, Ramasimong Phillip Tsokolibane, has demanded that his nation break completely and decisively with the British Empire. Former President Zuma—in turning to the East, to China's Belt and Road Initiative, and to the BRICS initiative of both Russia's President Putin and China's President Xi—had effectively moved in that recommended direction, but without speaking directly of the evil of the Empire,—until April 21. Observers on both sides of the imperial divide cannot help but notice the new congruence be-

Former President Jacob Zuma delivers his address on April 21.

tween what the LaRouche movement had been proposing and the remarks of the former President on April 21.

Within this growing ferment against the British Empire, the attack on the LaRouche South Africa website—reported in this issue (page 28)—must be located as a sort of pathetic and obvious effort of the Empire to strike back.

Mr. Zuma's remarks do not, however, bring the history forward to the present moment, in which a British puppet, Cyril Ramaphosa, has been installed in the Presidency. But as London and its thugs and pawns in South Africa fear, that is likely to come, as the global fight intensifies. In the meantime, anti-Empire patriots in

A portion of the audience at the event, sponsored by Black First Land First.

South Africa—and everywhere—can turn to this journal for their ammunition.

Video of former President Zuma's address, posted on the African News Network (ANN7) website, was suppressed within a few days of its appearance, and ANN7 itself has not survived, for related reasons. Here is EIR's edited transcript, with subheads added, of the first 36 minutes of Mr. Zuma's address—the portion in which he attacks the British Empire. EIR has now made the video of the entire address available, once again. Zuma was speaking at a "Blacks in Dialogue" event in Braamfontein, Johannesburg, under the sponsorship of Black First Land First (BLF).

Jacob Zuma: [video begins in mid-sentence] … was forced [by Governor Somerset in 1817] to cede land between the Great Fish and Keiskamma rivers to the British. As you hear, he [Xhosa chief Ngqika] was not asked, he was forced to do so. [applause] And they were doing it all over. One of the Zuma chiefs [had been situated] near Pietermaritzburg, the town called Howick,— all of that area belongs to the Zumas. We're claiming it! [laughter, applause] We're claiming it.

They came, the British, to say, "Look, we ask you to give a small portion; we want to establish a town." He said, "No. I don't want it." They went away. They came a second time with weapons and soldiers and guns, and said, "We have come to ask for this piece of land." [laughter] He realized this now was war, and said, "Well, you can just use that space only," as if that was not enough.

Once they realized how fertile the ground was,— You know this big dam, Midmar Dam, it's actually supposed to be Zuma Dam. [laughter, applause] After some time, they said, "No, can you just go to the other side of the mountain, so that here we will do something," and they were establishing farming. All those farms there, the majority of them, are British owned [inaudible].

Bambatha, a Zulu chief, led the last military action against the British occupation forces, in 1906. Here, Chief Bambatha (right) and an attendant.

The critical point is that they had every power we didn't have, to colonize us. We fought, though—seriously.

In 1818, the British invaded the Xhosa territory, by attacking Ndlambe, who was one of the leaders, and seized 23,000 cattle, marking the outbreak of the Fifth War of Dispossession. Subsequently, those Xhosas and those communities whose cattle had been seized, rallied behind Makhanda ka Nxele, who led an attack of 6,000 warriors on Grahamstown. They provoked us. They did everything.

In 1825, Landdrost [Cape Colony Magistrate] Andries Stockenström—or -room or -rome, I don't know [laughter]—begins issuing temporary permits allowing white farmers to graze their livestock north of the Orange River, but they were not allowed to trade or erect buildings. This changes later in the decade, as farmers stop asking for permission and simply inform the magistrate.

1828: Ordinance 49 of 1828 is passed. The ordinance allows the government to source laborers from "frontier" communities. All black workers were given passes for the sole purpose of working, and all contracts over a month long were to be registered.

So, systematically, they began to want to know each and every one of us. You must carry a pass, you must be registered, you must be known. [That was] partly also to prevent us from fighting, because they can easily identify us.

Annexation after Annexation

In 1829, January, Maqoma raids Bawana, a Thembu chief, forcing the latter's followers to flee across into territory seized by the colonialists. Stockenström got the expulsion of Maqoma from the Kat River Valley and establishes a settlement for landless Khoi, to create a buffer zone between the Xhosa community and white settler farmers, and to consolidate territories seized by the colonialists. Maqoma responds by increasing cattle raids on white farmers, forcing them to informally

The Battle of Blood River, 1838. Voortrekkers, led by Andries Pretorius, defeated the Zulu at the Ncome River and took possession of the area from the Tugela River to the Umzimkulu, to form the Republic of Natalia. In 1844, the British threatened Natalia and then took it over, renaming it Natal (see map).

allow him to return to the territory.

In 1833 and 1835, in December, the Xhosa community launched an attack on the British after [Xhosa chief] Xhoxho was injured by a British patrol, sparking the Sixth War of Dispossession.

So you can count a number of incidents where we were provoked. They covered, in actual fact, the entire country. They moved throughout, they attacked, [inaudible]. There are these guys, like Sir Benjamin D'Urban—I don't know why Durban was named after this fellow. [Inaudible] And there was annexation after annexation.

In 1837, voortrekkers [Afrikaners moving from Cape Colony to the interior to get free of British rule] under the leadership of Hendrick Potgieter defeated the Ndebele under Mzilikazi at the Marico River, and seized vast tracts of land between the Limpopo and Vaal rivers. It must be noted that Mzi-

General Sir George Cathcart, governor of Cape Colony, attacked the BaSotho people under King Moshoeshoe in 1852.

likazi is one king who was effectively exiled by the Boers and seems to have been written out of South African history. He had to cross to Zimbabwe finally; he went to Botswana, then crossed to Zimbabwe. And he had had quite a big kingdom.

In 1838, in May, the voortrekkers led by Andries Pretorius fought and defeated the Zulu at the banks of the Ncome River, called the Blood River, and dispossessed them of their land. In fact, they took the whole area in the south of the Tugela [River], naming it Republic of Natalia. It only changed later, when the British took it, and they called it Natal.

It's countless, the accounts where they went. They even went to the Sekwatis [royal family of the Pedi], particularly the Afrikaners went, Hendrick Potgieter. He also signed a treaty there. So there is no corner of the land they did not touch.

The point I'm stressing is that this was *long* before 1913. [applause] You can deal with many instances that will indicate that indeed, long before 1913, the land was taken—from everybody, to every community in South Africa. There are details that will always, in a sense, support this view. It is absolutely important for us to be aware of this, and I think we need, on this matter, to put our facts together, as the Black Caucus, instead of just demanding our land.

But let those among us who can put it together, and articulate it, present it everywhere. And I would be happy if you could go and address Parliament [applause] about those matters.

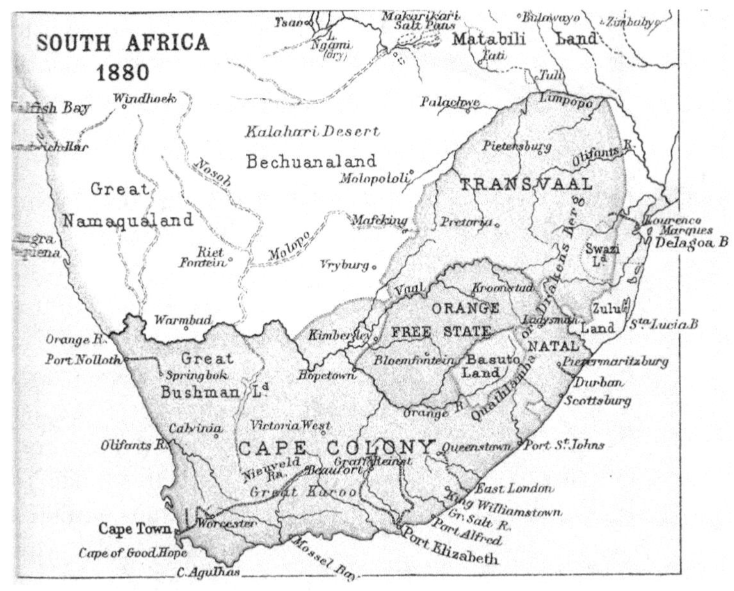

In 1848, in February, a government land commission established during the year, states that the extent of land recommended by the 1846-47 commission is excessive. The commission apportions land to white settlers.

This point about settlers is important for us to appreciate: Part of our difficulties in South Africa is because we have the biggest number of European settlers—in the whole world. [applause] And we've got to appreciate that therefore, the resistance to giving land is going to be very serious.

Many countries in Africa were colonies. Once they were decolonized, the administrators packed their bags and left. Here, we used to call it, Special—hmm? [audience responds, "Colonization of a Special Type"]. Exactly, Colonization of a Special Type, where the colonizer lives with the colonized.

That tells you how difficult our struggle is. In all other countries, they left, but the people remained, did whatever they wanted to do with their land, their everything. With us— different—we're all here. [laughter]

Creating a Docile Workforce

In 1850, Sir George Grey confiscated land from black people, leaving them to search for work on farms.

The taking of the land—one of the things that encouraged it, was to force blacks, particularly after the discovery of diamonds and gold, to go and work. If they had land, they would not have had to leave, and so it was important to deliberately dispossess them. There were many things they introduced, in order to force us to go and work, so the taking of the land created the labor force. We were people, in our country, citizens [indistinct], working our land, everything. We're then turned into laborers, because the land had been taken from us.

In 1852, the British under Sir George Cathcart attacked the BaSotho under King Moshoeshoe. And it was the same, until King Moshoeshoe asked the British to help.

King Moshoeshoe of the BaSotho (1786-1870) with his councilors. After repulsing the British and then the Boers, Moshoeshoe lost extensive territory to the Boers in new attacks. Moshoeshoe eventually turned to the British for protection in 1867. See Basutoland on the map (now Lesotho), an enclave within South Africa.

There are many of the incidents that detail how the land was taken away from us, and I don't know why people should pretend it never happened. [applause]

In November 1853, a resolution taken by the Volksraad [Afrikaner legislative assembly in the Transvaal] enabled District Commandants to grant land for occupation by Africans on condition of "good behavior." [laughter] And "good behavior" was simple: be kind to them, don't fight. However, under the resolution there was no individual title. Africans had to use the land communally. Chiefs were regarded as trustees of the tribe. However, power over the land still remained the hands

Illustrated London News, 1879

The British invasion of Zululand (north of Natal, see map), in 1879, led to the Battle of Isandlwana, in which the Zulu inflicted a humiliating defeat on the British. Here, two British officers retreat from the battle (seen faintly in the background). Of 57 British officers, five survived. The British lost a thousand rifles, their two field artillery guns, 400,000 rounds of ammunition, most of the 2,000 draft animals, and 130 wagons.

of the white government. "Be kind, the land is not yours, it's just that your chief is keeping it in trust." So, all of that.

In 1855, in June, Resolution 159 is adopted by the Transvaal government. It prohibits anybody who was not a burger [citizen] from owning land and also prohibits Africans from having burger rights. So there were laws and regulations made just to keep you away from land.

1856, voortrekkers declare an independent Zuid-Afrikaansche Republiek, and lay claim to the Transvaal,— You must not like my Afrikaans. My Afrikaans is prison Afrikaans. [laughter] It is very different.

They declare this republic, and lay claim to the Transvaal and the land up to the Limpopo River. [They] just say, "This is our land now. Move off."

Still, Whites Should Have Some Land

In 1857, in April, Lieutenant General Scott issues a proclamation offering vacant Crown lands which are between 300 and 3,000 acres. This increases land speculation by white settlers who, in turn, after pur-

chasing the land, lease it to Africans, at yearly rental of 5 shillings. So, with time, it becomes stronger and stronger.

In 1958, the First BaSotho-Boer War breaks out as a voortrekker commando attacks Thaba Bosiu. In response, the Sothos mobilize an army of 10,000 warriors who raid unprotected settler farms and defeat the voortrekkers and force them to retreat. This battle continued for some time, until Moshoeshoe asked for British protection, and then that's how Lesotho becomes the British protectorate, protecting themselves from the Boers.

This happened in every other area, until they covered the whole country. Kingdoms fell; some disappeared. After pushing some people across rivers, they put on the other side, the line of soldiers that are waiting for people to cross.

The story of land is a sad story in our country. It's a sad story that there was a deliberate decision to send a particular number of settlers in 1820-something, to come and settle and draw a border, to say, "This land at this site, now belongs to somebody."

When people send their cattle across, if they cross their cattle too fast, they are called "thieves": "They have come to steal our cattle." And I don't think they came with a single cow in the ship, when they landed. [applause]

The critical point is that the issue of the land needs to be discussed properly. We need to discuss it fairly. We are not saying these people should have no land. We say we can't remain without land, when they have land. We must find a formula. We tried to work out on a formula, willing something and willing something. [laughter] Willing seller, willing buyer.

Audience member: Willing buyer, willing seller.

The Battle of Ulundi, 1879. After their defeat at Isandlwana, the British attacked the Zulu anew at Ulundi, with a changed and reinforced order of battle, and prevailed. They captured and deported King Cetshwayo and broke up the Zulu kingdom into 13 chiefdoms.

Zuma: Willing buyer, willing seller. It did not work in the 24 years [since majority rule began in 1994], sufficiently. And we need to agree, rather than to say, "No, no. This can't happen; it's wrong." Because you make us think about this history, and to ask, then, what must we do? [applause]

In 1879, Zulu warriors defeated the British at the Battle of Isandlwana, January. The British forces are defeated by the Zulu *impis* [warrior formations], at the Battle of Isandlwana, indeed.

Africans Turn to Political Methods

In November, the Pedi under the leadership of Sekhukhune are defeated by British forces, leaving about 1,000 Pedi warriors dead. Sekhukhune is captured and imprisoned in Pretoria. Just look how the kingdoms,— which have been destroyed without any second thought.

In the Cape, the government annexes Fingoland (amaMfengu) and Griqualand West, which constitutes two-thirds of the territory between the Cape and Natal.

In 1882-83, white farmers lay a siege on Ndzundza (Ndebele) for nine months, who when faced with starvation, are forced to surrender. Their fertile lands are seized and divided among the voortrekkers. Each war participant is given five families to use as servants, who work for little or no pay on the farms.

So we've been turned into real proletariat, into almost slaves. You are sitting here with your land—suddenly it is taken away. Suddenly, your enemy says, "You are now my worker. I'll pay you if I want. If I don't—sorry."

1885: Gcalekaland and Thembuland are incorporated into the Cape Colony. So anything that was remaining, is taken.

1887: After defeating the Zulu warriors at the Battle of Ulundi [1879], the British formally annex Zululand to pre-empt the simmering threat of the Zulu people fighting back to recover the loss of their territory. The kingdom is broken up into thirteen chiefdoms by Garnet Wolseley and placed under different chiefs, each with a British resident. The chiefs are asked, and told, "The magistrate is your *nkosi* [master]. You report there."

This is a story of the land, how it was taken, and how we became landless.

The last one—there are many—the last one was the introduction of poll tax, which made Chief Bambatha rebel. Chief Bambatha kaMancinza, on his own [applause] led a bloody revolt and defeated the advancing British law and forces who were trying to fight him. [He] dealt with them, but they organized; more reinforcements were sent in to try and capture him. He fled and operated from the Nkandla Forest and continued to build a resistance army and conducted a guerrilla warfare, together with Chakijana.

The white troops in the area were faced with that fight, including the leaders, chiefs who agreed to pay poll tax. Chakijana had formed the guerrillas. They dealt with them. That led to the arrest of King Dinizulu and indeed, Bambatha was defeated.

This was the last resistance from us, as Africans. It

The British could not tolerate the existence of the Boer republics and provoked the First Anglo-Boer War against the South African Republic (Zuid-Afrikaansche Republiek, shown as Transvaal on the map), 1880-1881. Here, the British attack the Boers at Majuba Hill in 1881. The Boers prevailed, but conceded defeat in the second war, 1899-1902, and turned to political methods against the British.

sent a very clear message that the methods we have been using so far did not work, to make us defend our land. And made our forebears take a decision to fight differently, to use the political methods to fight, because *land* had been taken. This was a very serious situation, because in a clash between the Afrikaners and the British that led to the Anglo-Boer War, as it was called then, the main thing is that the land had become a big issue for the British. They did not want Afrikaners to have what you call the republics [the South African Republic and the Orange Free State], without *them* controlling. And that's why that war occurred.

No, Land Theft Did Not Start in 1913

And finally, the Afrikaners were defeated. They then put together a new country, the Union of South Africa. Now, if we say, by 1910, the whites, who were fighting among themselves, had reached an agreement to put together all four republics and make one Union: Why do we think, after 1910, the land was not taken away? [And that] it was only taken away in 1913 [by the Natives Land Act], and [that] that's

where we should claim.

I think it's an issue that we need to deal with, logically. Because it is the 1910 Union establishment which put all of us blacks out; only whites [had rights]. We had no vote, we had no participation in Parliament, in localities, everywhere. That's what made those who felt we now have to fight differently, to form an organization for the first time. And every, *every* community was represented in Bloemfontein [at the founding of the African National Congress in 1912].

And the issue was not alone just the land. The land, the country, in whatever form you call it, the authority, our rights—everything. In our country, we have been pushed out of administration. And this is what made us to say, "Let us fight."

Now, what is interesting for me, is that, at that time, those people who lived more than a century ago, made a call, that this problem is facing us blacks, that we cannot defeat the colonialists, if we are not united. If we think we can fight it, in our different things,— by that time there were few organizations that each of the provinces had, and they were convinced, we need to form one organization. We must *all* be part of it. We use it to unite all of us. And they said, at the time, let us stop— let us stop fighting among ourselves; let us stop the animosity among ourselves. [applause]

And that shows, when we are feeling good, we say these were "old people," who are not as bright as we are. We can now operate and manipulate high-tech things. Certainly we believe we are actually better than those. Hmm? [speaking in isiZulu:] *They couldn't drive cars. Even riding a bike, they would fall off.* [laughter] We fly planes today—but we can't see the sense that Africans must unite. [applause] That is my biggest problem....

IV. The Four Power Agreement

November 18, 2008

LAROUCHE WEBCAST

The Four Power Agreement In Its World Context

This is an edited transcript of Lyndon LaRouche's Nov. 18, 2008 international webcast from Washington, sponsored by the Lyndon LaRouche Political Action Committee. The moderator was LaRouche's West Coast spokesman, Harley Schlanger.

Schlanger: …As the present global financial disintegration has been unfolding, and accelerating, we've been hearing, constantly, the refrain: "No one could have known it was coming." That refrain, no matter how often it's repeated, is dead wrong. We're also hearing another refrain, as trillions of dollars are being pumped into dead banks, in a futile effort to save the bankrupt system: "No one knows what to do." Again, those repeating that refrain, are dead wrong.

It's my great honor and privilege today to introduce to you the one man who not only forecast this crisis, who knew it was coming, but has offered a solution, and is organizing globally to implement that solution:

Ladies and Gentlemen, join me in welcoming economist and statesman, Lyndon LaRouche.

LaRouche: Thank you.

What we're involved in today, is a general breakdown crisis of the world financial-monetary system. There is no possible rescue of this system, as such: that is, the present, international monetary system can not be rescued. If you try to rescue it, you will lose the planet. You have to choose: Replace the system, or get a new planet. Those are your choices, essentially. I think that any sane person would say, "Keep the planet."

Mars is not particularly hospitable these years; I understand it's rather cold there, at present.

So what that means, essentially, is, the world is now operating under an imperialist system, which is actually part of the British empire. Now, the British empire, is not the British Empire: It's an international monetary-financial system, which has a base in England, but which operates globally. And since the breakdown of the U.S. dollar, in 1971, and the subsequent launching of the highly speculative market in petroleum—the short-term speculative market in petroleum—the U.S. no longer controlled its own dollar. The dollar has been controlled increasingly, as the U.S. economy has deteriorated, by a London-centered crowd, centered in those financial interests.

The result of that, plus the fact of what was done, beginning in 1987, under a now departed—happily—former head of the Federal Reserve System, Alan Greenspan, is that a new addition was added to this process of this speculative kind of currency. It was based on a system which had been pioneered by a Michael Milken, who went to prison in the 1980s for what he did; but Alan Greenspan made it international.

So that, what happened last July, a year ago July, was not a crash of a short-term market, at all—a real estate market. The real estate market was collapsing, or did collapse, as I said it would collapse, exactly at that time. But there was no real estate market collapse of the type talked about. What was collapsing was the system.

Now, the system is in the order of magnitude of

EIRNS/Stuart Lewis

Lyndon LaRouche addresses the Washington audience, Nov. 18, 2008. "You have two ways to go," he said. "Either you collapse the world, with starvation and mass death, and those effects. Or, you put the thing through bankruptcy reorganization."

EIRNS/Stuart Lewis

more than a quadrillion dollars, many quadrillion dollars, of speculative currency, out there. More wealth nominally, than the world contains. Everything had been done to prop up this crazy dollar, as an international currency, controlled, not by the United States, but by a syndicate of international financier interests: the floating-exchange-rate system. And what happened is, they had gone into the area of U.S. real estate, as in London and elsewhere, in trying to create *debt*, synthetically, to cover this vast accumulation of unregulated dollar claims in the international market: quadrillions of dollars claims. Maybe more than $1 quadrillion. Maybe $10 quadrillion, or more than that.

And so, there is not enough money, real value in the world, to cover the demands against currency. And therefore, the system has gotten to the point, that under the present system, you've got to *sacrifice the currency claims*, or you've got to sacrifice the real economy. Which means, there's no way, that you can reorganize under the present world monetary-financial system. You have to put the whole system into bankruptcy reorganization.

Now, how can you do that? Well, what you can do, is end the existence of monetary systems: You put them into bankruptcy and close them out. Well, what do you do for money? We go back to the U.S. dollar.

The American Constitutional System

Our Constitution is unique among nations, in many respects: that we're a true nation-state, where European nations are not true nation-states. They may aspire to be nation-states—Charles de Gaulle tried to do that in France—but they're not really nation-states. Because they are under a parliamentary style of system, and a parliamentary style of system is inherently not a fully sovereign system of sovereign nation-states: It's controlled by something else; it's controlled by international monetary interests.

So, what we can do, is, very simply, is we can go back to the U.S. Federal Constitution, and create what's called a "credit-based dollar," as opposed to a "monetary dollar." A credit-based dollar is consistent with our Constitution: that no money, as legal currency, as legal tender, can be uttered under the U.S. Constitution, without a vote by the U.S. Congress on behalf of action by the U.S. Presidency.

So, in our system, the official currency of the United States, insofar as we follow our own Constitution, is limited to dollars, or dollar-equivalent negotiables, which are uttered *only* by previous authorization of the U.S. Congress, especially the House of Representatives, and uttered by the U.S. Federal government! There is no such thing as an international monetary source, which gives us our currency—not legally. It is uttered by the U.S. government; it is sovereign. We are a sovereign state, and our currency is uttered by us, under our Constitution: by approval of the House of Representatives, and by the Presidency. No other currency exists.

In Europe, that is not the case: In Europe, the monetary systems are *not* controlled by the government. They are created by central banking systems, which may negotiate with governments, and have agreements with governments, but the governments do not control the monetary system, as such. In point of fact, that is the *essence* of a free-trade system: that the governments have no essential control, as issuing authorities, over debt and credit outstanding.

And it's because of the utilization of that provision, that artificial money was created, by people making a capital promise, in capital amount, to go into debt, to get a lesser amount of money uttered in their behalf, now. That's how the world incurred a presently outstanding debt, through such means as derivatives, in the order of *quadrillions of dollars*! Far in advance of anything that could ever be paid. So, we are *never, never going to pay those debts!* We *couldn't* pay those debts. So, we're never going to pay them.

What do you do in a case like that? What does the United States do in a case like that, under our Constitution? You declare those debts *in bankruptcy*. And what do you do with them in bankruptcy? You sort them out! Those things that should be supported, will be supported, and the rest of it will just wait, or die away. The great majority, the vast majority of the obligations outstanding today, as nominal claims against countries, *will be cancelled*. Those things which should be paid, will be paid. Those otherwise, will never be paid. And they will never be paid, in any case!

A Four-Power Alliance

Now, you have two ways to go: Either you collapse the world, with starvation and mass death, and those effects. Or, you put the thing through *bankruptcy reorganization*. And how do you do that? Well, what I specified is very elementary: I have four nations in mind that can take the lead on this thing. And the four nations, which together, represent the greatest consolidation of power on this planet: These nations are the United States, Russia, China, and India, as joined by other nations, which join in the same deal. We put the world

through bankruptcy reorganization. How do we do it? We use the U.S. Constitution to do that.

The U.S. Constitution is unique in the fact we have a kind of Federal Constitution we have: that our dollar is not a monetary dollar; it's a credit dollar. In other words, the United States has uttered an obligation, on behalf of the U.S. government, which can be monetized. That is our obligation; that's our only obligation, and any other kind of obligation is not fungible.

Other countries have a different kind of system.

Now, if the United States says, that we are going to back up our dollar, and enters into an agreement with Russia, China, and India, to join us, with other countries, in doing the same thing, to put the world through bankruptcy reorganization, in which we will *cancel* most of the outstanding financial obligations: It has to happen. Otherwise, no planet! If you try to collect on quadrillions of dollars of outstanding claims, from whom are you going to collect, by what means, and what's the effect? It is *against natural law*, to collect on that debt! How many people are you going to kill, to collect that debt? How many countries are you going to destroy, to collect that debt?

So, we have this monetary authority outside, which has treaty agreements with governments, but which has no real obligation to governments otherwise, except the treaty agreement. This agreement has resulted in the creation of a vast world debt, a monetary debt, which can never be paid. Well, obviously, the system is bankrupt! You shut down the system, and put it into bankruptcy reorganization—it's the only remedy.

A Credit System

How does it work for us? Under our Constitution, any credit we utter, in a monetizable form, is an obligation under the authority of the U.S. government, in each process, by the approval of the Congress, the uttering of it, and by the action of the Federal government, with that approval. Now, also, not only do we utter our currency, properly, under those terms, but if we, as a nation, as a sovereign republic, enter into an agreement, a treaty agreement with other countries, for the same system, then under the treaty agreement, other countries enjoy the advantage of the same system we have for reorganization of our debts.

And that's the only way we can get out of this mess.

So, we create a group of nations, who are operating under treaty relationship with the United States, which

United States: Contour farming in Iowa, alternating alfalfa with corn, provides protection from soil erosion. American agriculture, once the world's best, must be restored.

A Four-Power agreement among the United States, Russia, India, and China is essential to reorganize the financial system and stabilize the world situation. These nations are each very different, and have unique problems and unique contributions to make.

An Indian satellite launch. India has a top-rank scientific and technological cadre force, dating back to the Nehru years.

China's Sun Yat-sen University. China is committed to advanced technology and educating its huge youth population, although it faces many obstacles.

Russia's Trans-Siberian Railway was built on the principles of the American System of economics. The nation is reviving an emphasis on infrastructure development, after long neglect. This image is digitized from a 1910 color photo, made on three colored glass plates.

gives Constitutional protection to this, so that we now have created a new system—a credit system—to replace the existing monetary system. And everything that is put under the protection of the *credit system*, is now solid. Everything else is thrown onto the floor, to see what you can pick up: It's in bankruptcy.

So therefore, we can create a new credit system, among nations, which I think—if the United States, Russia, China, and India agree, most nations of the world will happily join us, especially considering the alternative. And therefore, we can create a new world system, a new money system, a credit system as opposed to a monetary system. And under those conditions, we can proceed to advance credit on a large scale, for physical reconstruction of the world's physical economy. We can organize a recovery of the same type, which we undertook with President Franklin Roosevelt, back in the 1930s and 1940s. And we won't change from that, I should think, once we've done it.

That's the only alternative.

Now, what that means is, politically, the end of the British Empire; or what's called the British Empire. The British Empire is the present world empire. There is no other empire on this planet today, except the British Empire. The use of the "empire" to describe any other system, is incompetent. The British are the only empire, and the British Empire is that which controls the dollar, the floating dollar today, the monetary dollar.

So, under these conditions, we then proceed to world reconstruction. And what we do, instead of the present free-trade system, is we go back to a protectionist system, a fixed-rate system; in other words, currencies will have a fixed rate of exchange with respect to each other, or adjustable by treaty arrangements, but they do not float. And we then proceed to utter the credit, for large-scale infrastructure investment, which will be the driver of the physical reconstruction of the planet. *That's the only remedy.* Any suggestion but that, is insane. Any failure to do exactly what I've prescribed, is insane. All sane people will, therefore, immediately agree—or we will have to draw the obvious conclusion.

So, that's what I outlined, in essence, as to how this would work—that's the core of it. This is the U.S. Constitution. It's a system which worked, every time we've used it. If we go back to it once again, as we did under Franklin Roosevelt, we'll come out of this nicely.

Globalization: A Crime Against Humanity

What are we going to do, however? We have, then, a physical economy, which is a mess. We have a situation in which the people are in jeopardy, life is in jeopardy; the conditions of life, the *physical* conditions of life are deteriorating throughout the United States and elsewhere. We have a problem of starvation in many parts of the world. Much of the human population is now in desperate jeopardy, because of current food prices and current organization of food production. Globalization has become a mass murderer, and globalization is virtually a crime against humanity, in its present implications.

We set up a system, as you may have noticed, with the case of Monsanto and other ones, where we grow food in one country to be eaten in another country. And we don't grow food for that country, much in your own country. You grow food for other countries, under the present kinds of agreements, WTO type agreements, to produce food for people in other countries. For the food you eat yourself, you have to go to a completely different country than your own, and get them to produce food for you. In the middle stands someone who's a dealer in food, the international financial community, which determines the prices which are paid for the country which exports the food, and also determines the prices paid for the country that buys the food to consume it. And what we've done recently, is we have destroyed the independent food-producing capabilities of nations, so they no longer have self-sufficiency. They are at the mercy of something like the WTO, which is a form of mass crime against humanity! The WTO should be repealed, immediately; cancelled immediately! It's a crime against humanity, its very existence. People should grow food primarily in their own country, and get supplementary foods of special types they may require from other countries, where they're better produced. But the sovereignty of a nation, in respect to its own production and consumption of food, is primary. So therefore, that part of the system has to end.

Most of the other features of globalization have to end. They will end, if we're human, if we're decent. And that means a complete change of course from what the present trend in policies is. Most treaty agreements that now exist will have to be cancelled, relevant to this. And practices of this type will be outlawed. Food prices will be under international supervision, to make sure there's no more of this fraud.

You have to realize, that billions of people's lives are presently in danger, as a result of these WTO and related policies, the effect of them. That's our problem. And our remedy is to use great power on this planet, to force through a system, a fixed-exchange-rate system, to establish a credit system in place of a monetary system, and to launch large-scale projects through joint credit structures which finance these projects, which enable nations to build their way out of the present physical mess we have today.

It's a tough one. And people say, "Why do you want to do that? Couldn't you take *slo-o-w-er* steps? Slo-o-wer steps?" "Well, you know that train's coming down the track, and you're walking across it—do you think you should take slo-o-w steps?"

No. So therefore, what you need, is you need these four countries. And they are different countries, as you may have noticed, not only different as nations, but they have different characteristics. We have one characteristic, as the United States, when we're functioning properly. Russia has certain characteristics which are unique to Russia. China has characteristics, including social characteristics, which are unique to China. India has characteristics which are different than any of the other countries. But this is a great part of the human race, the population, totally. And you have countries that are associated with them, like Japan. Japan's market is principally Asia. Its best market, for its high-tech production, are neighboring countries of Asia, which include Siberia, include the mainland of China, and so forth—that region of the world. Japan has a high-technology capability, which is extremely valuable. Korea—especially South Korea, but really Korea as a whole—has also a very significant potential. Also Korea is different than Japan and China, and Russia, and therefore Korea is a very valuable country, in the sense that it's not the same as China, Japan, Russia, and so forth. And therefore, the cooperation among these countries of different characteristics is a very important stabilizing factor in the world situation. It also is a key part in production.

The Problem of Power-Generation

India has completely different characteristics in this respect, but it also has, in effect, similar problems. The most common problem, is power. Now, we have nuclear power, developed today. It's the only decent power, that we have for dealing with these kinds of problems. Because, you can not measure power in calories. Only an idiot, or someone who is ignorant would measure power in calories. That is, a kilowatt of sunlight, and a kilowatt of nuclear power, are not the same thing. You can not replace a kilowatt of nuclear power by a kilowatt of sunlight.

In the process of power, the low end of power is generally sunlight, as it impinges upon the Earth. That is a very poor quality of power. Now the best thing you can do with sunlight, is what we tend to do with Earth naturally. That is, sunlight has a very low cross density in terms of intensity, as it hits the Earth. The most useful thing that sunlight does, is it helps to grow plants. Now, how's it grow plants? Well, one case is, of course, the green plants. Take power in terms of being applied to green plants. Now, the green plant has something in it called chlorophyll. Now, chlorophyll has a wonderful quality: Is that the individual chlorophyll molecule, which looks like a pollywog under a microscope—it has a long tail which is sort of an antenna; and it has a head with a magnesium molecule in the head. And the sunlight impinging on this antenna is now captured by some of these molecules. The power which is obtained by this antenna-like section of the molecule, now powers the magnesium head complex of that molecule. These molecules interact together, and what it does, these collections of molecules in chlorophyll, is increase the energy-flux density of the power which it has absorbed by means of these tails, from sunlight. This high-intensity power then converts carbon dioxide and so forth, into oxygen, and carbon products, and living things. So this, in turn—the increase in chlorophyll—cools the atmosphere, gives you a more uniform temperature, it turns a desert into something else, and that sort of thing; and therefore, all life on Earth depends, to a great degree, on this action of chlorophyll: of converting sunlight, through the action of chlorophyll, into a higher order, which then feeds all kinds of living processes, grows trees, cools the atmosphere. It does all sorts of good things. And this process is now essential to the system of life on Earth, and developing the entire planetary climate.

If you go to solar energy as a source of something else, and take the sunlight and now put it into trying to heat something, directly, what're you going to do to the climate? You're going to increase the temperature of the climate? Because you're not cooling it; plants cool the climate, green plants. You're going to have a higher temperature. You're going to come to creating an *artifi-*

The pollywog-like chlorophyll molecule "does all sorts of good things": It converts sunlight into a higher-order energy form, feeding all living processes and controlling the climate. But don't think of using solar energy, where nuclear power should be used instead!

cial desert! Where you want a green planet, you are creating *a desert*. And you say, "That's better for nature." This is only from the mind of denatured idiots, who think of these kinds of things. That's why they're called denatured.

So, in any case, therefore, the key thing here, is to increase the energy-flux density of power. Now, how do we do that? Or how have we done it so far? Well, you can burn brush—that's not too efficient. Again, you're burning something that was once alive. Another way is to burn wood, as such—a little bit higher order of fuel. Or you have charcoal; now, charcoal is a little higher order in combustion, in terms of energy-flux density, than just wood. Or you can go to coal, which is more efficient than wood. You can go to a more efficiently condensed form of coal, called coke. You can go to petroleum, a still higher order. You can go to various kinds of natural gas, that's a little bit better.

You can go to nuclear power: Boy! A factor of a thousand times or more better! You can go to a high-temperature gas-cooled reactors—oh, you're getting up there, buddy! A high-temperature gas-cooled reactor of a pebble-bed variety, you can start to desalinate, in a great way! You can take and provide large masses of water, and create the conditions of life. Don't use petroleum the way you do it now: hauling cheap petroleum all over the planet at high prices, to burn it! You generate, from water, you generate high-temperature gases, which are much more efficient for airplanes and automobiles and so forth; and other kinds of synthetic fuels. Then we will go, at some point, to thermonuclear fusion, which is still tens and thousands of times more efficient than that.

So, in this process, we go to higher and higher degrees of man's power to shape nature, per capita and per square kilometer. So, by going to these greater energy-flux densities of power, we're advancing the condition of life on the planet, for mankind as a whole.

Now, what we obviously wish to do, is just exactly that. For example, in the case of India: India has a large supply, a natural supply of thorium. Now, thorium is a material which is related to uranium in its function, but it's generally not useful for making nuclear weapons; it's useful for producing power systems. India has the capability, with thorium, and with a large stock of thorium, and with thorium reactors, to increase the energy-flux density of its area. Now what that means is, you have in India, take a case, about 70% of the population is not too well trained, not too technologically qualified. But that's not going to stop you, because if

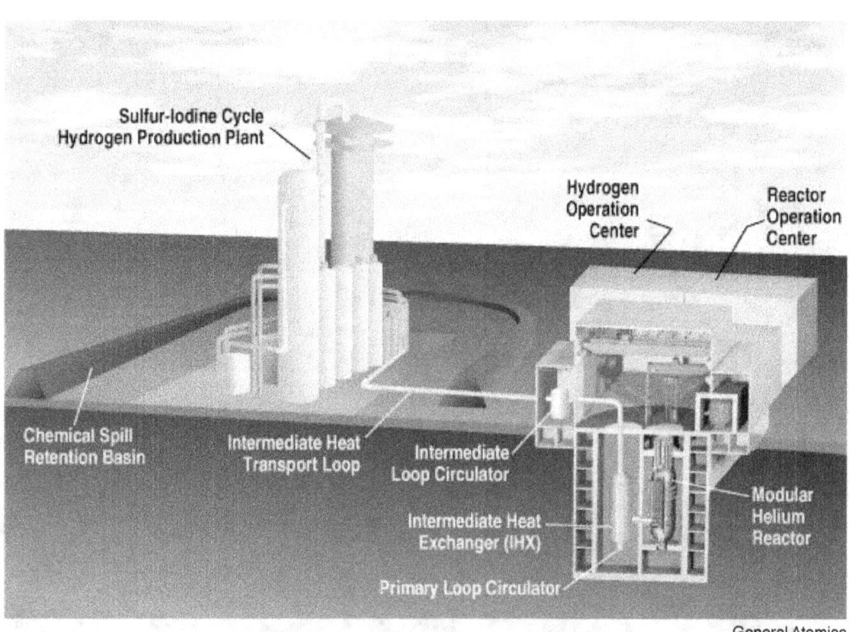

General Atomics

Institute of Nuclear Technology, Tsinghua University

The key thing is to increase the energy-flux density of power. Go nuclear! The best choice is the high-temperature gas-cooled reactor (HTR). Left: An artist's depiction of a proposed HTR reactor, coupled with a hydrogen-producing plant. Right: The bottom of the reactor core in a demonstration HTR in Beijing.

GNU/Michel Maccagnan

Thermonuclear fusion will be thousands of times more efficient even than fission power. Shown here, Korea Superconducting Tokamak Advanced Research (KSTAR), at the National Fusion Research Institute in Daejon, South Korea.

you can increase the power available, locally, per capita and per square kilometer, in a country, you can take the same quality of labor—which is not too efficient, because it's not skilled, it's not trained—but you can increase its productivity without yet changing the way it behaves. By power supply, you can provide water, through desalination; or other kinds of things. So you create an environment, an infrastructure environment, in which the same quality of effort, the same level of skill by an Indian worker in a village, can be increased by several times, several-fold; conditions of life can be improved.

So therefore, the general method we've used in humanity, in our successive ventures, is to improve the environment, the environment of production, which as a lever, increases the productivity of production, in human terms, in terms of human effect. Therefore, you *upgrade* the conditions of life, by concentrating efforts on improving what we call "basic economic infrastructure," that of art, agriculture, and industry, and city life, and things of that sort. And that's the way we have to go.

Save the U.S. Auto Industry?

For example, the question will come up; it comes up all over the place: Shouldn't we go back to making automobiles again? No! I fought for that back in 2005, and early 2006. The Congress of the United States killed the idea of saving the automobile industry, when I was about to save it. They killed it in February of 2006: Now, the same idiots, who killed the automobile industry and destroyed it in February 2006, are now

ABr./Antônio Milena

Washing clothes in a ditch in Mumbai, India. Many people fled poverty in the rural areas, flocking to the cities in search of jobs—which turned out not to exist.

WHO/P. Virot

Farming in Radjastan, India. Indian farming is being smashed by globalization, leading over 100,000 farmers to take their own lives in the last five years.

India's IT sector is no solution to the nation's economic problems. Here, a BPO India Call Center. American consumers are well acquainted with such call centers, which deal with everything from software viruses to broken washing machines.

saying they're going to come back and start producing automobiles again, having destroyed the market for, and the ability to produce automobiles! Simply because people want to manufacture automobiles, there's a form of fantasy life now! There's no sense for the United States to go back into the automobile industry, not at this time. It's insane! But it's attractive to people who don't think.

Why are the people who shut down the auto industry, in February 2006 when I was working to save it, or save part of it, and save the industry, as well as the automobile production—why do they want to start it up now? They shut it down! The present Speaker of the House was one of those who shut it down! She says she's now promoting it! Did she change her mind? Did she change some other things? It's all fakery.

What we need now, is not U.S.-produced automo-biles—the Japanese are doing a fine job of more than filling all our requirements. There is an excess of automobile production, en masse, throughout the world! Why are we going back into the automobile manufacturing business? To produce vehicles we can't sell? Just to look at them?

Well, let's try something else: Let's take the highways around here. What's the congestion: How much time do you lose every day in commuting to work in the Washington, D.C. area? What is it, two hours commuting for you? Two and a half hours each way? What are the tolls you pay on these routes? How much of your personal life is lost by this commuting—as opposed to what you would have, if you had a high-speed rapid-transit system network to transport you, without having to drive the car, without having to smell the other guy's gas, ahead of you. You're getting sick.

How much would you like to have more time for family life? If you're spending five hours a day commuting, what kind of family, if you have two adults, both working, and some children: What kind of a family life are you creating, for Americans with that kind of arrangement? Shouldn't we have, instead of all these automobiles on the highway, with all these tolls, and all these fumes to smell from the automobile in front you—wouldn't it be better to get a shorter, and faster transportation system? And to have a better family life? Maybe a few hours a day saved, for some kind of normal family life, not wondering what your children are doing all these crazy hours?

Don't we have a shortage of clean power sources? Don't we have a shortage of investment in manufacturing things that we need, which we're wasting on this sort of stuff?

And, do you have clean water? Do any of you remember the time, you could get safe, fresh water, out of a city water system, from a tap? Do you remember

The German-built maglev in Shanghai, China. High-speed rail is the best solution to the congestion of highways in the United States and other countries. The technology exists, so why not build it?

Transrapid

getting "toll house cookies"—you never get toll house cookies in tollbooths! So, it's consumer fraud. We don't need that: What we need is an environment which is largely a free environment, because that's not the way to have commerce; but an environment which is not just free, but it becomes an essential part of providing the environmental conditions of life, in which the productive powers of labor, per capita and per square kilometer, are increased.

So, in many parts of the world where you have poor people, as in Africa, with no infrastructure, and other parts of the world like that, you're not going to get a significant increase in productivity by applying the effort to the local point of production. You're going to increase the productive powers of labor, by providing the infrastructure, which enables the existing level of personal skills to be much more efficient in terms of their effect.

when that was? How many bottles of bottled water do you drink a day? How much does it cost you? How much did it used to cost you, the same amount of water, safely out of a tap?

Build Vital Infrastructure, Worldwide

So, what you need—the conditions of life and the conditions of production; we have a shortage of infrastructure in this country, of basic economic infrastructure. Not infrastructure like sidewalks, to pay taxes on! You have people in New York, like this crazy Mayor of New York: He wants to take over the infrastructure. He'll buy your sidewalk, and he'll put a tollgate at each block! This is not what I mean by infrastructure!

What you need are the basic things, like a generally *free* transportation system! We don't need the tolls! We don't need the tollbooths! They're not digestible. The story about

David Shankbone

EIRNS/Ryan Milton

The LaRouche movement in New York City rallies against the fascist policies of New York Mayor Michael Bloomberg (inset), Oct. 30, 2008. "Mouseolini" Bloomberg is giving the Fascist salute. If Bloomberg had his way, he'd put a tollgate on every sidewalk!

Kill the bugs, in Africa! Maybe some food will survive. Africa is one of the largest food-producing areas in the world, but most of the food doesn't survive to get to somebody's mouth. The diseases are not controlled; you don't have the transportation systems in order to connect communities, to provide the services which are needed for agriculture.

What we need in the United States, and other parts of the world, is the basic development of improved infrastructure, as it affects human life and production, in order to increase the productive powers of labor per capita. That's what we need in the United States. We need to increase the productive powers of labor. At the same time, we have a population, which, over the past period, over the past 40 years!—40 years! *Forty years!*—the United States has been losing productivity per capita over 40 years. It started back in 1967-1968, we began to lose, shrink, net infrastructure development: Over the course of time, we lost our industry, we lost our productivity, we lost science, we have people doing kinds of work that is not work any more, just make-work to keep them busy; and services, to service services, to service services. We destroyed that! We have a people that no longer have the *skills* to produce what they used to be able to produce with the same population then, today. We've lost that.

We have been insane *for 40 years*! Since 1967-68, Fiscal Year '67-68. We have been losing infrastructure. Under Carter, we had a disaster! We wrecked the U.S. economy under Carter! That was Carter's great achievement! Under the guidance of David Rockefeller, with the Trilateral Commission. We've been destroying the United States! We've been destroying Europe! Look at Germany, since 1990: The economy of Germany was destroyed, on orders from Margaret Thatcher, Prime Minister of England; supported by George H.W. Bush, the father of the present idiot; and the support of Mitterrand. Germany, which was a powerhouse of productivity, has been virtually destroyed by this order. Similar things have happened

Germany, which used to be a powerhouse of productivity, has been virtually destroyed since 1990. Here, a closed factory in Berlin.

EIRNS/Ilya Karpowski

The end of communism in Russia in 1991, and its replacement with "free-market" oligarchism, destroyed most of what remained of the nation's productivity. Russia's leaders are now trying to restore it. Here, a woman sells goods at an open-air market in the 1990s.

in the rest of Europe: Poland is much worse off, today, in terms of productivity, than it was under the Warsaw Pact. Other countries of the former Comecon states, are similarly situated. We destroyed Russia, in terms of economic productivity. We destroyed essential parts of the productivity of the entire planet; we destroyed technology, with these measures.

And therefore, we have great needs for breakthroughs in technology, which are within our reach; but we also have to be able to assimilate technology, by

The United States used to have a balance of agriculture, infrastructure, and industry, dispersed throughout the country. Now, family farms have been replaced with centralized cartels, and former farm belts have turned into wastelands. Here, a Missouri rice farmer.

what? By improving infrastructure: the infrastructure which is necessary to enable labor of a certain skill to improve its productivity, because we have unskilled people! We don't have the skilled labor population we had 40 years ago! We've lost it! We have a very small fraction of that. We're about to lose much more of that, right now.

Look, take the aircraft industry—we were talking about this today. We have, most of the modern planes that we're developing, aren't flying! We're flying old planes, of lower technology. We've lost the technology that we once had, or the relative technology that we once had. So we've got to back to that, and dig up that. So, what we need is the large employment, that's feasible, for the development of the basic economic infrastructure which is needed to increase productivity per capita. And to then use that, to gradually phase in the population, back into the kinds of production levels we used to have, when we had the skills to do that.

So, putting money into automobiles that you can't sell, hmm?—which you can not compete in productivity with other countries which are producing automobiles, because our capability—we were doing it already before we shut down the automobile industry; while Japan and Germany, especially Japan, and Korea, were increasing their productivity in the area of auto and related things, *we weren't*. We were using old technologies, to produce so-called "new, modern" cars. We can

no longer compete with Japan or Korea. We lost it—that was a deliberate choice, a policy choice.

So what we have to do, essentially, today, is we have to think in these terms, go back to a high-energy-density policy. If you don't believe in nuclear power, you're an idiot. You're not going to succeed. You have to go back to a high energy-density system of infrastructure. Stop all this highway building! Get back to mass transit.

We also have an insane policy on development of the economy generally. We used to have the idea of taking every state of the Union and developing production in every state: In other words, you spread production and its skills throughout the United States. That was one of the functions of our developing of a national transportation system. You didn't have super-industries where the whole industry was concentrated in one corner of some state and not in others. We had a balance of agriculture, infrastructure, and industry, which we used to develop the separate states of the United States, at least to a certain degree. So we distributed the productivity over the countryside. We didn't try to get giant industries to gobble up all of these things.

So we would balance the cost of production against the economy as a whole, this whole territory.

We were doing, essentially, with many wrong things included, but relative to today, what we were doing 40 years ago, was sane, compared to what we're doing today, which is relatively insane. And our first objective is, to do what is immediately feasible, is to recapture the kinds of things we used to do, and do them once again. And measure what we assign people to do, to what the present skills are out there.

One of the first areas we have to get into, is the system of education: Our public education system stinks. So you've got to get back to an education for human beings, not for monkeys. And often emotionally disturbed monkeys, is what we're doing today: We're turning children into emotionally disturbed monkeys, which creates a market for teaching children who are emotionally disturbed. And the training program itself, increasing the disturbance. That's what we're doing.

So we have to get back to the standards we used to practice, and realize that we've been systematically destroyed by the policy-changes which have been in effect over a period of time.

Roots of Our Problem: British Fascism

This goes way back, and we have to remember how this happened: In the 1920s and the 1930s, before the election of Franklin Roosevelt, coming out of the First World War, the leading financial powers of the world, were headed toward global fascism. That was the policy. Germany did not create fascism; Britain did. Hitler was put into power in Germany by the British, with help from New York City, people, like the grandfather of the present President of the United States, Prescott Bush. Prescott Bush was the guy who personally issued the order, which refinanced the bank, and refinanced the Nazi Party in the end of 1932, to enable Hitler to become dictator of Germany in January of 1933. And these guys, including that crowd, including Prescott Bush, remained on the Nazi side, up into the time, we ourselves were going to war against Nazi Germany. And he got into trouble at that time.

Truman was also involved in that kind of stuff, back then.

The whole Wall Street crowd was just as Nazi as the British were, and the British created Hitler. It's absolutely clear. They created Mussolini. Winston Churchill was a backer of Mussolini, up until the time that Mussolini invaded France. And Winston Churchill was still his friend, even after that. Winston Churchill was still supporting Hitler, until Nazi Germany invaded France.

So Hitler was not a creation of Germany; Hitler Germany was a creation, largely, of London, with support from a lot of people in the United States—including from the grandfather of the present President of the United States, Prescott Bush.

So, what happened in this process, is, Franklin Roosevelt, in becoming President—over the objections and the opposition of the financial crowd of J.P. Morgan and Co., which supported Hitler and had supported Mussolini—Roosevelt produced a miracle of saving the world from going into a fascist dictatorship, then. And the British finally agreed to go along with him, when Hitler invaded France, and broke the agreement that Britain had with Germany in support of Nazism.

So, what we did, in my generation, in going to war against Hitler, and in setting up what Roosevelt intended should become a post-war development,

changed history for the better. But the moment that Franklin Roosevelt died, we were in trouble! (I was there; there are a few, maybe one or two in this room, who were there at the time, who were adults at the time, as I was.) And they moved as fast as possible, as time would allow and public toleration would allow, to move back in a different direction: Back to exactly the policies that Franklin Roosevelt had opposed, back in 1932-33.

And that's the root of our problem.

So today, when I am proposing what I'm proposing now, which sounds to anybody looking back on those days, as exactly—I'm proposing to go back to the kind of philosophy of outlook that Franklin Roosevelt represented, back then, in '32-33 and afterward.

I'm going against them, kicking against the pricks.

Because the trend is what? The trend has been continuously one toward *world fascism*. That's what's been happening in this election campaign, so far this year. A drive toward a new kind of world fascism, called "globalization."

Therefore, if you look at this, look at the process by which we have been destroyed from what we were becoming, and had become, up until the end of the last war, especially since 1968 to approximately '71. If you look at that, you see, this is not some "natural" process: This is the natural *consequence* of an intentional direction of policy in the wrong direction! We didn't collapse because we were worn out; we didn't collapse because the environment was strained; we didn't collapse for any of those reasons! We collapsed because somebody intended that we should be collapsed! Because they wanted *their* kind of society, the kind of society they were headed toward, under Wall Street influence back in the 1920s, into the early 1930s. And we had a replay of that, right in the recent election campaign! A replay of 1932. Only in that case, Roosevelt won.

So, we're in trouble today, only because we made that change—and we've made it again, back in the same direction.

We're Going Straight to Hell!

Now, the question is: Do we want to survive? If we want to survive, we have a lesson of how to survive, in what Roosevelt in particular accomplished as President, during the time he was President. We can survive. But, if we don't, we're not going to survive. As a matter of fact, with the present conditions, if those changes are not made, you must expect that there will never be a recovery of the economy: *This present crisis will be a permanent one.*

We now have between 6.5 and more billion people on this planet. Two generations from now, we will have less than 1 billion, something like the dark ages of the 14th Century. And if we continue in this direction, the direction we're going in now, the direction which we're going in as of the 18th of November, the direction we're going in as of the end of the week—if we continue in that direction, that's where we're going: We're going straight to Hell!

And the alternative is, to turn this around. Go back! Recognize: *We're headed straight toward Hell, right now!* This is not somewhere down the line: We're talking about this year—we're talking about January, February. This joke that was passed this week [at the G-20 meeting], this joke with this President of the United States, this silly fool! And the silly fools that were participating. Many people were not silly fools there, but they said, "We're going to go along with this, because this guy's getting out of here. It's temporary." If we go in that direction, we're finished. Civilization as you've known it is finished.

It's happened before! Look at the history of mankind in total! Look at what we know about the history of mankind. This has happened before! Not exactly the same thing, but the same type of problem! Mankind had a civilization which was on the way up: The conditions of life of the average person were improving; the culture was improving; technological-scientific progress, in terms of those times, was going on! Mankind was on an upward course!

And BOOM! Something like this intervened. The civilization went into a crisis, and collapsed. It's happened repeatedly. Dark ages are a characteristic of mankind, at every part of mankind. In every case, there was the possibility of not letting that happen. In many cases, it was allowed to happen; no one resisted.

Are we now going to resist? Do we care what happens to our people, what happens to the country in the coming period, what happens to the world? Are we willing to kick against pricks? Are we willing to say, "No, no, no! You don't do this to us"? Do we have political leaders who have the guts to do what's necessary? Do we have political leaders who have even the guts to *recognize* that it's necessary, even if they don't have the guts to do it?!

We have people, who tell me, "Well, can't you com-

promise? Can you start this a little bit here? A sample, a teaser here? To see how it works?" When you're on the ship that's sinking? The *Titanic* is sinking, and you want to argue about stateroom accommodations?

That's our situation now.

Use the Presidential System

So therefore, that's what I laid out on Tuesday, last Tuesday. It's an outline of exactly the policy we can follow. If we can reach agreement, in the United States—I don't care who the current President, I don't care who the President-elect is. We have a Presidential *system* which is more important than any President: Can the *Presidential system* of the United States decide to reach an agreement with Russia, China, and India—*now!*—to take joint action, which will turn the planet around. And that joint action *would turn the planet around!*

Are we willing to do that? With the understanding that we're going back to the kind of policy that Franklin Roosevelt represented in his time, that we know we must represent, relative to our circumstances in our time? If we're willing to do that, and if we can engage Russia, China, and India, which are countries completely different in culture than our own, and different than each other; if we can engage in that, with those four nations, and others, to make a commitment to say, "This is not going to happen to us: We're going to take action to transform this planet. We're going to move upward," we can survive, we can succeed. Are we willing to do that? If we are, we can survive. And if we're not, we're a bunch of fools! And richly deserve what's going to happen to us, if we're not willing to do that. That's the issue.

And people say, "Well, explain your scheme, explain your scheme." I say, "Look, it's simple: You guys are a bunch of fascists. Now, stop being fascists!" That simple, just stop being fascists. Don't pull these swindles, you're stealing, you swindled everything out of our people!

What do you think the debt is that the typical American has? Look at the quadrillions of dollars of debt out there! Don't talk about subprime mortgages! The so-called subprime mortgage is the fag-end, a little, teeny fag-end result, of the big one—which is *quadrillions of dollars*! You're going to walk into some poor householder and say, "You owe a quadrillion dollars?" The guy's going to say, "Take the house!"

No, that's the point we're at: We've got a bunch of

cowards, and they're not stinking cowards, because many of these people who are acting like cowards, by combat standards are cowards; by ordinary standards, no. They're just frightened people, who are afraid of taking on a tough enemy who they know is a killer. George Bush is a killer, you know. Look at how many people he killed. How many people, how many Americans did this guy kill, in wars that should never have been fought? In other effects on people, that should not have occurred; he's a killer. He'll kill you—willingly. Won't even care.

And that's the problem: People in power *know* that! Not just George W. Bush, but other people in power, are just as bad, or worse. George Shultz is worse! He's a more mature killer. Felix Rohatyn, who was one of the supporters of the Pinochet regime in Chile, is worse. One of the big funders of this Democratic campaign— George Soros—is a killer. One of the biggest drug dealers in the world. A mass murderer: Who took his experience in sending—he's a Jew, remember—sending Jews to death camps, as his job, as a teenager: And *with the same mentality, unimproved*, conducting similar operations, today.

So, the guy out there, the politician who looks a little bit frightened—don't necessarily call him a coward by ordinary standards of cowardice: Take into account the fact that he's terrified. He's not combat worthy, or combat ready. And therefore, he's frightened; he's running scared. He's a deserter, in fact. And some deserters had a good excuse, didn't they? They were frightened.

So that's our part—and some of us have to stand up, as I'm doing, and take leadership in this situation. Because, if we do it, we have in our hands the ability to introduce the policies that will succeed. If we bring together, cooperation among the United States, Russia, China, and India, and other countries follow and join that, *we can turn this world situation around.* We can get back to something which is going in a different direction—we can do that. And the question today, is, are we willing to do that?

Look to Future Generations

The problem today, is a question of morality of a special type: When I was younger—and some of you, who are approximately my age, or verging upon it, were younger—when you thought about life, you generally thought about two generations of preceding generations, grandfather and father's generation; and you

How many Americans did President George W. Bush kill, in wars that should never have been fought? Shown: The burial of Staff Sgt. Nathan J. Vacho of Ladysmith, Wisc., who was killed in Iraq on May 5, 2006.

thought about two generations to come, you thought about becoming a grandfather, and the two generations that would come afterward. Many people who immigrated into the United States thought that way. They came here as poor people, from poor countries, or poor conditions in other countries, and they looked forward to their children succeeding and their grandchildren succeeding. The idea of coming over to the United States, as labor, in New York City, and ending up with a grandchild as a scientist or a doctor or something. It was a sense of achievement and that was the mentality of people from that time, people coming to this country as a land of opportunity to become something, to develop into something.

That's not the standard today. The standard is much more selfish. Self-centered is, "When I stop breathing, I don't care any more." In my generation, or in older generations, that was not the standard. We said, "I'm going to stop breathing, but what I'm doing is going to go on. The process I'm part of, is going to go on." And therefore, you weren't a dog, you were a human being. And like a human being, you thought in terms of coming generations, as well as past generations; you thought of how you had come into being, you thought about your background, you tried to learn from your family's experience, and the experience around you of older generations; you tried to see where the country's going; you tried to see what role you were playing in the country; and thinking about raising a family, and seeing what comes of that family two or three generations from now. And life was organized around this kind of idea, of family and community. Of a meaning of *being* somebody, and who you were in a community that's growing and evolving with successive generations, about four, five, six generations, was the context of your life.

And if you did a little study of history, you would look back further, a few hundred years; or if you studied as I did, you'd look back a few thousand years. And look

The Grand Coulee Dam, in Washington state, with Lake Roosevelt behind it. The enormous dam is the fourth largest producer of hydroelectricity in the world, and all the Pyramids at Giza could be put inside its base. President Franklin D. Roosevelt authorized its construction in 1933, and it was completed in 1942.

ahead at least a couple hundred years. And you situated your life, in what your role is *now*, in the time-phase you occupy in life—relative to a few thousand years before you, and maybe a hundred or more years to come.

And that's where you located your interest! Your interest in *being*, was not what you experienced while you were alive. But what you experienced in knowing what you were part of, in times past and times to come! What you were determined to help *cause* to be the case, in times to come! It's like the grandfather who would take his grandson out to a large project, like the Tennessee Valley project of the old days, and saying to the grandson, "I helped build this. See what I helped build." And that was the standard of life.

The problem today, is that standard doesn't exist. It exists in rare people; it exists to some degree in a feeling and anticipation of desire; it's the desire to be human, the desire to have a sense of immortality. But there's not much substance to it. There's not much confidence in it, because the society doesn't encourage you to think in those terms.

And so that's the situation before us. We can solve this problem, and discuss it here. We can solve these problems: But we have to understand the problem. We have to understand that we are now at the end of civilization. That the policies which are being presented to us, by high-level sources in the United States, in Europe generally, lead to an absolute disaster for humanity in the very near term.

There is no question whether this system is coming down or not! It is coming down, now! And without the kind of radical changes that I indicate, this system is coming down this year! This year and the coming year. It's coming down: It's gone! There's nowhere else to run to! You want to live in Hell? Stay where you are. No need to change, no need to travel: Just stay where you are, it'll come to you.

But, the point is: Are you willing to take the risk of changing? Are you willing to fight the war that has to be fought, rather than some war you would rather fight?

That's the situation today. That's my situation. You've got to think in those terms. I've spelled this out in writing, I've spelled it out in the past weeks' time, in several ways, in a number of pieces. The situation is clear to me, we can win, it's possible: But, it's not likely, is it? You have to make it likely. Maybe some of us have the guts to do it.

www.ingramcontent.com/pod-product-compliance
Lightning Source LLC
Chambersburg PA
CBHW080242260726
48658CB00008B/3201